"With a breadth and scope of a writer who has lived her message as well as written it, Emily Freeman's *... Little Ways* will capture your mind and ... fresh vision of the life you were ...

—**Mark Batterson**, *New ...* ... r of
...aker

"Emily Freeman's luminous words hand you your rightful birthright: to be as creative as your Creator Father. Read them and exhale. These pages just might really wow you awake to who you are meant to be . . ."

—**Ann Voskamp**, *New York Times* bestselling author of
One Thousand Gifts: A Dare to Live Fully Right Where You Are

"I read this book during a time where my art, my writing, felt more like wrestling with lions than soaring with creativity. Quite simply, I wanted to put down my pen and walk away. But Emily's words ignited something new and fresh and invaluable deep within me. Let this book help you release the art you were made to create and live!"

—**Lysa TerKeurst**, *New York Times* bestselling author;
president of Proverbs 31 Ministries

"This book is a word painting, a shout from the rooftops, that deep within each of us, we all are God's poetry—the butcher, the baker, the candlestick maker, the housewife, the sculptor, the newspaperman, the carpenter. This book scares me a little, because it makes me ask myself not, *what if I'm not an artist*—but, *what if I am?* Emily has an extraordinary gift, and she shares it with us in this remarkable book."

—**Tsh Oxenreider**, author and blogger at SimpleMom.net

"Dear World, Prepare yourself. Enjoy your last day of being filled with fear and guilt and wondering if what you do really matters, because this book will forever change the way you see everything you do from the mundane nightly dishes to your most risky creative endeavor. I've been waiting all my life to read these freeing words."

—**Myquillyn Smith**, The Nester, author of *The Nesting Place*

"Emily Freeman is one of my favorite artists and speaks with authority, calling out the artist in all of us. Don't read this unless you're willing to be moved and rethink what you know about art, faith, and humanity."

—**Jeff Goins**, author of *Wrecked: When a Broken World Slams into Your Comfortable Life*

"I'm tempted to say that if I'd been handed this book of Emily's twenty or thirty years ago, I'd have written many more songs and shared them sooner. The idea that I am a poem and so are you, together God's masterpiece, that all of this life is a **walking installation piece**, changes the way I think of living, breathing, loving, writing, and singing. It's gorgeous and freeing, and most importantly, it's *true*. And as if the arrow-to-the-heart message of hers weren't enough, the *way* Emily carries it home with phrases that read like *song* lyrics makes every single paragraph a pleasure for the artist in me. She calls me out and up, and articulates the soul of my own struggle with art-making and sharing, even after years of doing it. She makes you want to shine. I'm personally deeply grateful that this book exists and have added it to my short list of must-reads for artists."

—**Christa Wells**, singer/songwriter

"Emily Freeman is one of the most gifted writers I have ever read, and *A Million Little Ways* is an extraordinary achievement. In this delightful, insightful, and life-giving book, with deep faith and a gentle sense of humor, Emily speaks openly, honestly, and directly of the journey to knowing and becoming one's true self. This passionate book penetrates the soul, and it will challenge you and inspire you in the most wonderful of ways."

—**Fil Anderson**, author of *Running on Empty* and *Breaking the Rules*

*a million
little
ways*

Books by Emily P. Freeman

Grace for the Good Girl
Graceful
A Million Little Ways

a million little ways

uncover the art
you were made to live

emily p. freeman

Revell

a division of Baker Publishing Group
Grand Rapids, Michigan

Published by Revell
a division of Baker Publishing Group
P.O. Box 6287, Grand Rapids, MI 49516-6287
www.revellbooks.com

Printed in the United States of America

Library of Congress Cataloging-in-Publication Data is on file at the Library of Congress, Washington, DC.

ISBN 978-0-8007-2244-9 (pbk.)

The author is represented by Fedd & Company, Inc.

13 14 15 16 17 18 19   7 6 5 4 3 2 1

In keeping with biblical principles of creation stewardship, Baker Publishing Group advocates the responsible use of our natural resources. As a member of the Green Press Initiative, our company uses recycled paper when possible. The text paper of this book is composed in part of post-consumer waste.

For Dad—

You taught me to see beyond *what is* to *what could be*.
Thank you for connecting the dots.

contents

who is the artist?

You want to know the meaning of life? This is your highest calling: You are called into the dynamic co-creation of the cosmos. This breath is your canvas and your brush. These are the raw materials for your art, for the life you are making. Nothing is off limits. Your backyard, your piano, your paintbrush, your conversation, Rwanda, New Orleans, Iraq, your marriage, your soul. You're making a living with every step you take.

—Jon Foreman

1

awake

Art is when we do work that matters in a creative way, in a way that touches [people] and changes them for the better.[1]

—Seth Godin, author and entrepreneur

She was twenty when I first saw her, old enough to look up to but not so old I couldn't relate. I walked into the youth room of Highland Park Baptist Church late that night so the program had already started. Michigan winters didn't lend themselves to much inspiration, so when I saw her sitting up front leaning against a stool, her deep-set, mysterious eyes holding more stories than she ought to know at so young an age, I knew something was about to happen. Her generosity was palpable. She picked up her guitar, her small frame nearly disappearing behind it.

And she began to sing.

Her lyrics dripped heavy with questions and faith and love and longing. She didn't just sing notes, she sang *story*.

I came undone.

Listening to Sarah Masen sing that night, the winter before I turned eighteen, I thought it was her voice and her talent that touched me so deeply. I was aware of a mysterious movement within me, but I was unable to define it.

And so, I did what most people do. I believed it was her skill that moved me. That night I wished more than anything to have a talent like hers. I grieved the fact that my singing voice was average, my painting skills didn't exist, and my dancing was limited to jerky, stiff cheerleading moves.

I had heard talented musicians before. But this time was different. She offered herself honestly and beautifully, sharing something from within her laced with courage and hope. She showed me beauty and woke up a longing in me to take part in it. The beauty she shared was, quite simply, herself. And in sharing herself, she showed me a glimpse of the glory of God.

Decades later, I'm circling around that winter night in Michigan, realizing what was stirred up in me and knowing it matters. Technicians don't move us. Artists do. Skill may be impressive and even necessary, but skill alone doesn't touch the soul. The profound gift Sarah gave me was the recognition that it wasn't her skill that moved me, it was her *art*.

Sarah introduced me to a shadow of my true self, touched something in me that was there but sleeping. That's what artists do. They pull back the covering on our inner life, allowing us to see things beneath the surface, things that, without their compassion, creativity, and generosity, we may have missed.

The song lyric.

The exchange between actors on the screen.

The image of Paris in the snow.

The tuning of the strings before the show.

Art coming from honest hands shows us beauty, stirs up longing, and touches us deeply.

But what about this:

The extra care the cashier takes with your order, the way she looks you in the eye, asks how you are, if you need help or a price check, as if her work is important *and she knows it.*

The teacher who makes history come alive, telling stories filled with facts and truth and background, while students learn without even realizing it.

How many times have we been rushing through the day, weary from the world, grieving a loss we didn't even know we were grieving, and all it takes is for a stranger to offer to carry our bags from the baggage carousel to the curb and we break down as if they offered to buy us a house or bring our loved ones back from the dead?

Cashiers and cellists are capable of making art because they both have the power to influence, to be fully awake to their Maker, and fully aware of his making of them.

 I can't imagine anything more dangerous to the enemy of our hearts than people who know who they are.

Maybe you have in your mind a moment in time when you have been moved by the heart of an artist—you remember a second grade teacher who woke up in you a love for reading, a best friend who supported you in the midst of college drama, a musician who offered himself so fully to his audience that you couldn't shake the feeling for days after the concert.

It's easy to point out the influence in others, to see them as images of the Divine Artist, to be liberal with our admiration, compliments, or even our criticism.

But what of your own influence? What about the conviction of your true self, pointed out, accepted, and poured out as an offering?

Maybe you are a person who thinks art is for other people. Maybe you can't imagine God having art in mind when he made you. Maybe you doubt the connection between the work you do with your hands and the story you are telling with your life.

All of that has a particular time and place, right? Art is for a certain type of person doing a certain type of thing.

Art isn't for you.

Is it?

Could it be true that you, too, are an artist?

And if it could be true, wouldn't you want to find out what that might mean?

You don't need a test or an expert evaluation or an extensive and professional analysis to find out what kind of art you might have to offer.

You don't need to gear up for a long journey or take time off work.

Instead, I hope to do for you what Sarah did for me—pull back the layers suffocating the truth of who you really are.

Maybe you have a dream or a desire to move into the world, something you're always talking yourself out of. Or maybe you *wish* you had a way to influence others but you don't think you do.

It is my intention to introduce practices to help you uncover the art already alive within you.

You were born to make art.

But that's not all.

It is also my intention to walk with you as you begin to release your art into the world, for the glory of God and the benefit of others.

Because you were also made to live art.

It's time to rescue our beautiful design from the dark grip of doubt and discouragement.

It's time to remember the Spirit of power and love and a sound mind who lives within us.

It's time to live as though we believe we have something to offer.

It's time to release our authentic selves into the world.

Because it isn't only the painters who are allowed to be expressive, it isn't only the musicians who can touch our souls, it isn't only the novelists who can inspire us to dream.

Have you noticed how God does things?

Have you considered the way he colors the sky? Or the smallest details in the blades of grass or grains of sand beneath your feet?

Is he only a God of right answers and right angles and acceptable behavior? Have we exalted *the will of God* and *the plans of God* above God himself?

He does not manage us, to-do list us, or bullet-point us. He loves us. Is *with us*. And believing him feels impossible, until we do, like a miracle, like lukewarm water turning merlot red right there in the cup. And hope sprouts new, because God doesn't give us a list. He invites us into the story.

God is not a technician. God is an Artist.

This is the God who made you. The same God who lives inside you.

He comes into us, then comes out of us, in a million little ways.

That's why there's freedom, even in the blah.

Hope, even in the dark.

Love, even in the fear.

Trust, even as we face our critics.

And believing in the midst of all that? It feels like strength and depth and wildflower spinning; it feels risky and brave and underdog winning.

It feels like redemption.

It feels like art.

2

reflect

All earthly things are the shadows of heavenly realities—the expression, in created, visible forms, of the invisible glory of God.

—Andrew Murray, *The True Vine*

It's pink outside. I only know because the silver car in the neighbor's driveway is pink. Not the bubblegum kind. Not the kind mixed up in cans, but the kind that comes from heaven.

The sunset kind.

The car isn't the sunset, but it's telling me a story about the sunset all the same.

Those who have been gifted with the skill of a painter or a singer or a world-class dancer are living images, life testimonies, witnesses to the transforming power of art. They reflect the glory of God like that pink car in my neighbor's driveway, and they do it whether or not they know it. We respect and admire the art coming out of them. And we should.

Painters, dancers, and musicians may have more practice or natural inclination toward accessing their inner depths and sharing themselves with others. But that doesn't mean you must be able to paint, dance, or play the piano in order to share something of yourself too.

What about your banker, your accountant, your mother, or your waiter at that restaurant Friday night? What if *you* are the banker, the accountant, the mother, the waiter? What about the art of your soul? Is what you do simply *a necessary job*?

It may be hard to imagine we have something beautiful and creative to offer if we haven't a voice to sing or a hand to paint.

Perhaps those who make art in the ways we traditionally think of art give the rest of us a framework from which to live our lives. They offer a gift of knowing what life could look like if it were handled more like a mysterious piece of art rather than a task-oriented list. We may not all have the same skill or training as do the painters or the musicians, but we all bear the image of a creative God.

In coming up with a working definition of an artist for the purposes of this book, perhaps we could say, then, that being an artist has something to do with being brave enough to move toward what makes you come alive.

Art means believing that the God who created the world with words alone creates with words still, through us—whether it be on a stage to thousands or in a corner with one.

Maybe you make paintings, or maybe you make pie.

Maybe you live confidently in the midst of scary situations.

Maybe you are brave enough to listen, to wait, to trust.

Maybe you see potential in situations and in people that others aren't able to see.

Art is what happens when you dare to be who you really are.

You have the power to influence, to move, to make, to become.

You have the capacity to perform the human act of making art, of doing work that comes from deep within you and touches something deep within me.

We make art with our lives.

When a mother who thought she had no voice begins to realize her voice matters, a student who believed he was biding his time to live life for real begins to discover the life in today, a writer begins to tell her story, a servant opens his hands, and a believer finally believes—*art comes out.*

When we live free, we are able to give freedom. When we live loved, we are able to give love. When we are secure, we are able to offer security. God reveals himself through every artist, and the artist is *you.*

The question isn't *who is the artist?* The question becomes *who are you?*

We Bear His Image

Trees have always fascinated me. They are so confident, so sure of their identity. Feet rooted strong in the ground of their birth, they don't wander off to find out where they came from. Instead as they grow, their roots go farther into the ground where they already are and their branches reach up higher to God.

South Carolina is home to some of the most audacious trees I've ever met. These old men with their mossy gray hanging beards seem to behave all wrong for trees. They have trunks, and that seems right. But here is where the rightness ends. Their branches start at normal places, but then reach out, around, twist and tangle all the way to the ground, out nearly as far as the tree is tall.

It's as if they've spent a lifetime declaring God's glory, but their arms grew tired. So they found another way to worship, to reflect the glory of God. It's different, but no less beautiful.

These magnificent oaks were born of God's infinite imagination.

He spoke and it was. He speaks and it *is*.

Every good story begins with the story already happening. So when God said, "In the beginning," we know that wasn't the beginning of God. It was the beginning of *us*. It seems important, then, to consider how he decided to begin the story he's telling.

In the beginning, God made art. His art marks the foundation of everything we know. The kind of art God makes is not an afterthought or a weekend hobby he does on the side.

God's art is the starting point for the story of the world.

He spoke the world into being and there was light and dark and elephants and rivers and dirt that I wash from my son's fingernails. He spoke, and grass came out. He whispered lilies, camels, honeysuckle, and sand. Mountains were shaped by the timbre of his voice, and valleys swooped down low when he finished his sentence.

The first thing we know about God is he made art.

What is the first thing we know about people?

We were made in the image of God.

As lovely as creation is, we were not made in the image of a sunset or a snowcapped mountain or a Low Country oak.

When he spoke, the world appeared.

But when he breathed, he made man in his image.

Breathing—the sign of life.

My mom used to walk into my room when I was supposed to be sleeping, and stick her index finger under my nose to "check on me." My earliest rebellion was to hold my breath for as long as I could, just to see what she would do.

Breath is the evidence of life. So when God breathed, he put life into man. And he, the plural of God—Father, Son, and Spirit—decided that this man and woman with life in their lungs would bear his divine image.

"So God created human beings in his own image. In the image of God he created them; male and female he created them" (Gen. 1:27).

The Father, sovereign and holy; the Son, creator and redeemer; the Holy Spirit, comforter and indweller—this three-in-one God made man and woman to be like him, to reflect his image, to have a community relationship that mirrored the relationship of the Trinity, to declare his glory.

All God's work was good.

But man and woman are the *very good* of creation.

Genesis 1:26 begins with God creating man and woman in his image and it ends with God giving them a job to do.

The kind of creating God does is the kind *only* God can do. But he invited human beings to join him as co-creators. Not as equals with him, but as image bearers of him, to carry his image into the world.

"Then God blessed them and said, 'Be fruitful and multiply. Fill the earth and govern it. Reign over the fish in the sea, the birds in the sky, and all the animals that scurry along the ground'" (Gen. 1:28). They were made to be image bearers first and to do their good work out of their image-bearing identity.

But their understanding of their image-bearing identity came into question when Eve talked with the serpent and Adam stood silently by. The enemy challenged their identity. Bearing God's image no longer seemed to be enough. They wanted to be an *exact representation*. They didn't just want to reflect glory, they wanted to have glory of their own.

When they traded their identity, it messed up their work.

We Have a Job to Do

This is where a lot of us get stuck. As we begin to uncover those endeavors, passions, and pursuits that make us come alive, we have to remember the battle that will always ensue within us. Apart from God, we want glory for ourselves. There will always be a pull, a dark and desperate attraction to be God.

If we trade our identity, it will mess up our work too.

Jesus has always been central in the making of humanity, our only relief from our dark capacity to glory-grasp. He was there in Genesis as he is here with us now. The same way he made man and woman in his image in the beginning is how he is forming us now. The coming of Jesus reestablishes our identity.

In Genesis, God made us as image bearers with a job to do.

Now, look at Ephesians 2:10. "For we are God's master-piece. He has created us anew in Christ Jesus, so we can do the good things he planned for us long ago."

In Ephesians 2, we are a masterpiece made to do good things.

Sounds similar to Genesis 1, where God made man and woman as image bearers with a job to do.

So what does it matter?

These English words used in the text—*masterpiece*, some-times translated *workmanship*—these are translations of the original word used in the letter to the church at Ephesus, the Greek word *poiema*. Our English word *poem* comes from this same Greek word. Workmanship, masterpiece, poem—all these words in Scripture are used to describe God's work—you and me.

God calls you his workmanship, his *poiema*. What happens when God writes poetry?

We do. We happen.

We are walking poetry, the kind that moves, the kind who has hands and feet, the kind with mind and will and emotion. We are what happens when God expresses himself.

If we are made the poem of God, then what is the job he gave us to do? What is the job of a poem?

The text says we were "created . . . anew in Christ Jesus, so we can do the good things he planned for us long ago." The NASB translates "good things" as "good works." When I see

25

that phrase "good works," I tend to think along the lines of action and accomplishment. I'm programmed to think that means something it doesn't—something like *work hard to please God*. I am desperate to focus and do my good work because that part seems important. And it is.

But remember the two things it says before *good works*. The first thing I've already mentioned—we are God's workmanship.

The second thing? *We are created in Christ Jesus*, on purpose, *with purpose*.

Adam and Eve were made in his image and given a job to do.

You and I are remade in Christ, and we're given a job to do too.

But, this type of work we are to do is not the kind that comes from the outside, like a task we discover or approach. It isn't a talent or skill we go to school to perfect. This word for "work" is the type that assumes the completion of an inner desire.

When a poet writes a poem, he isn't writing a technical manual or a how-to booklet. A poet writes to express an inner desire.

We see that same idea here in Ephesians 2:10, where it essentially says, *You are a poem written inside the person of Jesus Christ. You exist to carry out his inner desire. This is your good work.*

So this is our job, to carry out the inner desire of Christ. And the inner desire of Christ is to bring glory to the Father.

Glory, the kind that comes from God, poured into his Son, placed into us, reflected back to him through the art of our life. We are here first as a poem to display the glory of God. He was pleased to have the fullness of his glory dwell in Christ, and equally pleased to have Christ dwell in us.

At the most basic level of our identity, your job and my job is to be a poem, the image bearers of God, made to reflect his glory. The art you and I were born to make is released out of the core of who we truly are, where our spirit is joined in union with the Spirit of God. Any movement coming from that place reflects the glory of God. This is our highest purpose and, ultimately, our greatest joy.

When the Poem Forgets Her Purpose

But things are not as they should be. We're desperately afraid of desire, terrified that if we consider for too long what we most deeply want, we will be confused about which desires come from us, which ones come from God, and how to tell the difference. (We'll talk more about desire in the next chapter.) We live in a fallen world with fallen people in a dirty mess. We are fallen image bearers, feeling guilty for things we ought to embrace and embracing the things that ought to bring guilt.

We may be displeased with the ways he wants to reveal his glory through us because they don't look like the ways he reveals his glory through others. We're uncomfortable with the implications and become confused about our own desire.

We are colanders filled with glory-water. Our best efforts are spent trying to cover the seeping holes with not enough fingers. God's glory demands display. Yet sometimes when we get a glimpse of it, when we taste something we come alive doing, when we feel that sense of purpose wake up within

27

us, we become terrified. And so instead, we spend our time looking for plastic bags to catch it before it pours out, wasted.

We want to be something more sensible, more practical. Something like a jar with a lid. No holes. No glory leaks.

Let's control it, contain it. Let's be reasonable.

In this action, we have forgotten who we are.

Surely God has another way to display his glory. Surely he doesn't intend to do it through me.

Is there anyone else in all of Scripture who can declare glory like a living, breathing poem? There is only one other place this exact word *poiema*, or *workmanship*, is used.

> For ever since the world was created, people have seen the earth and sky. Through *everything God made* [*poiema*], they can clearly see his invisible qualities—his eternal power and divine nature. So they have no excuse for not knowing God. (Rom. 1:20)

The earth and sky declare his glory. It's easy to agree that the heavens are the poem of God, the earth and all it contains. The tree stands where it is and lifts up arms to declare the glory of God. Or if it's a Low Country oak, it reaches out and twists around. But the credit for the beauty still belongs to God.

Heaven and earth declare.

But the people on earth despair.

Our own poetry is broken in the frailty of humanity.

So the Poet himself stepped out of heaven and into the poem, onto the dusty trails of the earth and into the desperate ruts of our souls. He steps out of heaven into us, his *poiema*, his workmanship.

And from the inside of us, he declares his *own* glory.

This is the most powerful kind of worship. This is what it means to be fully alive. Trees may declare God's glory, but they do not bear his image. Jesus uncovers our remade image-bearing identity and invites us to release our glory-declaring capability.

Being his workmanship doesn't mean we are all poets. It means we are all *poems*, individual created works of a creative God. And this poetry comes out uniquely through us as we worship, think, love, pray, rest, work, and exist.

Jesus reminds us we *are* art and empowers us to *make* art.

There isn't only one right way to do the job of glorifying God. There are many ways, *a million little ways*, that Christ is formed in us and spills out of us into the world.

Knowing you are a poem doesn't confine you to be artsy, it releases you to be you. We are art, every one of us. No matter our personality, skill, talent, or inclinations. The essence of being human is that we were made by design with the hands of the Divine Artist.

Christ came to reestablish our identity, showing us what it means to be fully alive as a human—how to live on earth as we were intended to live—a life of complete dependence on the Father. He lived as an exact representation of his Father as he fulfilled the law, saved the world, made wine in water pots and blind men see. He lived as a son, a brother, a friend, a teacher, a carpenter, and a savior.

He took walks and spoke with prostitutes and told stories.

He fished.

He laughed.

He wept.

He did all of this in the energy and by the leading of his Father.

But he didn't do all of that so we would have an image to copy. He sent his Spirit to live within us to empower us to be fully alive ourselves. He continues to do all of those things now *through us*—the will of the Father, the sacrifice of the Son, the energy of the Spirit—the creation work of the Trinity never stops. God is on the move.

But he is not invisible. As long as there are people on earth, the world will have glimpses of God. He chooses us to move through. He chooses your personality, your spunk, your passion, your strengths, and your weaknesses to work in and through and with.

Christ still moves around in the world through the filter of your you-ness.

And so the meaning of our lives is not dependent upon what we make of it but of what he is making of us. As we begin to grasp what that means, the words of God and the truth of Christ become less like words to live by and more like truth to live into.

This book isn't an attempt to redefine art.

It is a genuine effort to re-imagine our lives.

What makes us come alive goes deeper than what we choose to do in our professions and our free time. What makes us come alive is *life*, and this life is Jesus. Painting, cooking, parenting, calculating, and conversation all have the potential to hold within them a mystery and an expression of our life in Christ. This is the kind of art that combines the outward work of our hands with the inner workings of the soul and spirit, woven together, whole and complete and equally important.

Like the tree that grows where it's planted, we need not launch a search party to discover who we are. Stay right where you are, as you are, complete in your identity as an image bearer, and reach up your arms to God, reflecting his glory with your life.

But what does that *look* like? We'll spend the rest of this book uncovering your art-making, image-bearing, glory-declaring capability.

A Glimpse of the Glory

Boarding a tiny plane in Colorado Springs on my way home from a visit with friends, I stand single file in the aisle behind fellow travelers. Counting in my head, I see the only open window seat toward the back. That must be mine.

I crowd my way past the man in the aisle seat, an awkward exchange as they always are. Here is where we'll sit with one another for the next two hours, so close we'll both need gum, and I don't even know his name.

Will he be all closed-eyed napping? Newspaper reading? Flight-attendant flirty?

Turns out he is chatty, and a few minutes in, I realize I'm enjoying myself.

We make small talk because that's what you do, but when the plane takes off, I remember how much I hate these heavy metal birds. I'm pleasantly distracted by his talk about his work. "I make and fix trains for a living."

The train-maker's face lights up when he says it. In my mind, I see him as a five-year-old boy kneeling next to his dad's Lionel train set in a dimly lit garage. Maybe he wears a conductor's hat. He definitely blows a whistle.

His face comes fully alive with talk of the trains. He continues to tell me about his son and his wife and his face does the same thing.

I can't measure his passion for his work against his passion for his family just by looking. But I can tell they both bring him great delight.

This man's job is to make trains, to take metal and dream it into a moving, heaving locomotive. It seems to me train-making and train-fixing are part of this man's art.

Back home, when the red-and-white sticks fall slowly down over the road, I roll my eyes at the inconvenience. I have places to be and I don't want to wait, but here comes a train, so now what? I pull out my phone and check my email. I don't even look up as the stock cars pass, the railways carrying heavy cargo from one distant place to another. I ignore the work of the train-maker's hands.

But this train exists and runs and it does so because train-makers make it their job to make and fix the trains. A broken-down train can't sit there for long in the presence of the train-maker. His job is to make the train work, to run well, to reach its full potential.

His job is to reveal the full glory of the train.

Isn't that what artists do? They struggle and labor to express the full glory of what they want to say, how they see the world, the beauty that lives in their head? They do the work of getting it out of their head and sharing it with us.

What full glory does my life labor to reveal?

What does it look like to embrace the truth of our image-bearing identity and live into the job we've been given to do? Does that look different for you than it does for me? How?

I don't harbor lofty notions of expertise, as I'm not convinced there is such a thing in deep matters of the soul and spirit. But I hope to prove myself a worthy companion, an intuitive observer of the art of God. Still, there is one thing I know for sure: I know you are an image bearer with a job to do. And the simplest description I can come up with for what that means is this: You *are* art and you *make* art.

And the only place to begin uncovering what your art looks like is to start right where you are. Let's follow the arrows to your soul.

PART
2

uncover the art you were born to make

The gospel is life. The gospel is about the Creator God, who is an artist, who is trying to communicate. And his art is the church. We are the artwork created in Christ Jesus to do good works. If we don't realize that fully, then the gospel itself is truncated; and art itself suffers.[1]

—Makoto Fujimura

As a fellow image bearer, I want to whisper wake-up words into your spirit, where your life is joined with God's.

Wake up to the life of Christ within you and see how he wants to come out.

Wake up to your unique calling and live into the truth of who Christ is and who you are in him.

Uncover the art you were born to make.

Release the art you were made to live.

This is the gospel, the good news, the new way.

Here's a question you might be asking: What if I do the work of uncovering and it turns out there isn't anything within me worth offering?

Translation: *What if I look inside and discover I'm a hot mess?*

Can I go ahead and answer that for you? You are. You are a mess. You are and I am and everyone else is too. Some of us do a better job at hiding it than others, but it doesn't make it any less true.

Uncovering your art does not mean you will find only rainbows and sunshine to pour out on everyone around you. Uncovering your art is about uncovering what is really there within you, coming face-to-face with your profound capacity for beauty as well as sin, your deepest dreams and your longing for God.

You are capable of glory-grasping and it might get ugly.

But you are designed to reflect the glory of God, and when you release the fullness of who you most deeply are, we will see God because we're finally seeing you.

Uncovering your art is about waking up.

Being a mess doesn't disqualify you from having an influence. And it doesn't make you any less of a poem.

So instead of asking, *What if there isn't anything in me worth offering?* let's ask this instead: *What if there is?*

36

What if all that about you being a poem, about you being made in the image of God for a purpose, what if it's undeniably true?

If it is and you don't do the work of recovery, then you are really missing out. In turn, so are we. Because you are a gift worth offering, and if you don't know that, we're missing out on you.

There's a reason I chose the word *uncover*. It's because our image-bearing identity is already true. But we often cover it up with discouragement, doubt, practicality, or excuses.

Instead of setting off on a journey to *find* your art, consider staying right where you are to *uncover* your art. Like the tree with roots crawling deep into the ground, God has already done the work of putting his art within you. I believe he's asking us to do the work of uncovering what is already true and trusting him to release it for his glory and the benefit of others.

In the next five chapters, as you begin to consider uncovering the art within you, I want to suggest five places to look:

Look Within—What is it you truly desire? It's time to wake up to that.

Look Back—Where are there hints of your design hidden in your childhood? It's time to rescue those.

Look Up—Where is your true hope? It's time to sink into God.

Look Around—How are the critics causing you the most discouragement? It's time to see where your real life comes from.

Look Beneath—What moves you from the inside out? It's time to listen in a way you haven't done before.

3

desire

Look Within

> When we pay attention to our longing and allow
> questions about our longing to strip away the outer
> layers of self-definition, we are tapping into the
> deepest dynamic of the spiritual life. The stirring
> of spiritual desire indicates that God's Spirit is
> already at work within us, drawing us to himself.[1]
>
> —Ruth Haley Barton

Soon after my first book was released in the fall of 2011,
I had someone ask me if I thought that was the book I
was born to write. Part of me wanted to declare with
great certainty, "Yes! This is what I was made to do! This
book is the culmination of my purpose on earth."

But I couldn't say that.

I believe that book was the book I was born to write *for that particular season in my life.* Seven years before that book released, I brought twins into the world, revealing God's glory by being a mother (I still do that, by the way). Four years before that, I learned sign language and revealed God's glory by being an interpreter (I no longer do that at all). Just this morning I revealed the glory of God in my kitchen, making cookie dough.

If history is anything to go on, then one thing I know for sure is, the job I do with my hands will change over time.

I don't believe there is one great thing I was made to do in this world. I believe there is one great God I was made to glorify. And there will be many ways, even a million little ways, I will declare his glory with my life.

God did the work of making the world before sin ever entered the picture. He called his work good—in the case of man and woman, he called it *very good.* God enjoyed the process of making art and he delighted in the work of his hands. He then told Adam to cultivate and keep the Garden of Eden, a job requiring labor. It wasn't a punishment or a burden. Work was part of God's original design.

As image bearers of God, what does that mean for us? How are we to know what things we should or can pursue? Maybe those things bringing you joy do so because they are one of the *many ways* in which God wants to declare his glory through you.

That's something important to uncover.

Desire Defined

Throughout your life you may be able to recall many different endeavors that have brought you great joy—standing barefoot on an East Coast beach, sun warming your face and your heart; finally learning to ride a bike during the summer before first grade starts; walking down the aisle with the love of your life, toward your future and a weeklong honeymoon. You may have always had a desire to sing, to teach, to fall in love.

But there are other desires that aren't as obvious as these. When you're a kid, you don't want to go to the doctor because doctors give shots. Your bottom line deepest desire? *Avoid shots.*

But when you grow up and are able to think beneath the surface, past the pain and discomfort, you know shots may actually prevent you from getting sick. You may not enjoy the shot, but your *deeper* desire is to stay healthy. As an adult who is capable of seeing the deeper purpose in the situation, you honestly desire to be healthy. And sometimes that means shots.

As we begin to consider those things that make us come alive, it might be easiest to start from the surface and work our way in. It's easy to know what I desire on the surface— comfort, happiness, and acceptance, to name a few. Those desires are not bad things to want. But as a believer, there are desires that make a heavier imprint on my soul than merely being comfortable or happy.

Uncovering desire is the practice of learning how to look farther beneath the surface than we may be used to doing. It may require time, space, and solitude to allow our souls to become quiet enough to settle into what is most true. Learning to look beneath the surface is an important step in uncovering the art we were born to make.

C. S. Lewis wrote a short essay called *First and Second Things*. Here is a summary of it in a letter he wrote to Dom Bede Griffiths in April of 1951: "Put first things first and we get second things thrown in: put second things first and we lose *both* first and second things. We never get, say, even the sensual pleasure of food at its best when we are being greedy."

In other words, it's okay to want to be healthy, influential, and accepted. But if those desires become rights you clench in your hand, demanding they be met in your way and in your timing, you will never receive the satisfaction from them that you so desperately seek.

Where I've run into the most confusion, though, is wondering what it actually means to bring glory to God as a first-things pursuit. It isn't just me on my knees in an empty room with my hands lifted in the air. It can be that, but it isn't only that, and I would dare to say it isn't usually that.

How are human beings to reflect the glory of God in the world?

I have been tempted sometimes to throw every single desire I have into the "second things" pile for fear that they are things I'm making up. I tend to assume if it's something I really want, then it isn't something I should be allowed to have. Am I just being selfish? Greedy? Crazy?

It takes courage to honestly consider desire in the presence of Jesus. Am I brave enough to acknowledge what I most long for? Am I willing to expose my desires in the light of the love of God?

As we begin to uncover the desires we may be reluctant to face, remember the gospel makes it possible for us to confront whatever we see. Christ is intuitive enough to sort out the first and second desires on our behalf.

But first we have to know what they are.

Desire Uncovered

I like to read a book for writing inspiration by Natalie Goldberg called *Writing Down the Bones*. In it, she says first thoughts have tremendous energy. These are the things we actually see and feel before our rational and logical selves edit all our first thoughts out. In other words, there are things we *think* we should see and feel, and those are the things we say out loud rather than what really is. It takes time to uncover what our first thoughts are.

To get to those first thoughts, she introduces an exercise common in writing practice where you make yourself write for a specific amount of time. The only rules?

- You can't stop
- You can't cross out
- You can't worry about punctuation or grammar
- You must lose control
- You must not be logical
- If something comes into your writing that scares you, *you must dive right into it*.[2]

It frustrates me how difficult this exercise is. It should be easy because there are no rules (except the rule that there are no rules). But it isn't easy, at least not for me. The gift of this writing exercise is that it gets me to honest places I haven't always felt free to explore.

Isn't that interesting? It takes time to uncover our *first thought*. First thoughts can be scary, weird, raw, but also extremely sacred. We have to wade through the muck of our own manners to be able to look them in the eye without blinking.

I was in my late twenties the first time I ate alone at a sit-down restaurant. I showed up with a book for company and the waiter asked me when I walked in, "Party of one?"

As he said that phrase, a different phrase popped into my head: *Happiness, party of orange*. If you asked me how it felt to eat lunch alone that day, I would translate my first thought for you as something like, "It was nice!" because *Happiness, party of orange* doesn't make any sense.

That unusual, stray thought doesn't have much impact on my life. But when we're talking about desire—the ways we feel most alive moving around in the world—those things carry some weight. Sometimes, though, they make about as much sense to us as *Happiness, party of orange*.

When we aren't able to translate what makes us come alive into our own language, the temptation might be to dismiss it altogether. Many of us have spent our entire lives editing out our first thoughts. We do this for all kinds of reasons—to avoid critique, prevent failure, please people, or simply because we can't see how they will logically fit into our lives. So we tuck away our first thoughts, or in this case, our deepest desires, and we cover them up with more acceptable pursuits.

We can take this same writing exercise and use it as we begin to bravely consider where the art is alive within us. To begin to uncover those things that make us come alive, we need to practice getting to our first thoughts.

I'm taking a bit of a risk in asking you for a couple of first thoughts—after all, I just told you it often takes time to arrive there. But I'm wondering if you would be willing to give yourself permission to answer these questions in the most honest way you can. Here's the first question:

When is a time in your life when you felt most fully alive?

[handwritten margin notes: accepted team relationship Decide to move, ...]

Consider those times and spaces when that was true for you. Don't edit anything out. Grab onto those first thoughts and dare to hold them in your hands for a bit. Then answer this second question:

> When you feel most fully alive, what words or phrases come
> to mind that describe that experience for you?

Consider the answer for yourself, and then read some answers I received when I asked my blog readers this same question.

Awake	Strong
Light	Energy
Real	Grounded
Released	Complete
Delight	Joyful
Full	Glory
Free	Real
Open	Made for this

These are lovely words, words I want to describe the work I set off to do and the way I live my life. But all of those words don't paint the complete picture, because that wasn't all my readers said. They also said words like this:

Scared	Unraveled
Desperate	Nauseous
Terrified	Breathless with fear
Nervous	

As we begin to uncover the art that is already alive within us, there will be a mix of emotions and experiences that rise up to the surface. But that is what happens when you dare to uncover what is hidden deep within you—you don't necessarily get to control what you find. It's like an old, heavy rock in the backyard that has long sat on top of a buried treasure. There may be dirt and worms and roly-polies. But the treasure is still worth the risk of uncovering.

You have to uncover the art before you can release it. The problem for most of us is, we have let the negative emotions decide for us that the art isn't worth uncovering. We have allowed the terror of exposure and the risk of failure to outweigh the truth of our remade identity.

Desire Reclaimed

Her comment came on a Tuesday in response to a post I wrote on my blog. She spoke of her college degree, her marriage after graduation, her beautiful children, and her full life. She spoke of her responsibilities and her lack of time.

And then, in the PS she spoke of desire.

I have always wanted to write again—haven't much since childhood . . . Every time a friend writes something, I wish I were doing that.

I wrote her back and simply asked what was keeping her from writing.

Her honest answer: *This season of life won't necessarily afford me the pleasure of indulging in my wildest dreams.*

It was as if she was saying to me, "Look, I'm a grown-up now. I don't have the time or the luxury to consider what I most long for." She used the phrase "wildest dream" to describe her idea of writing. Wild dreams are usually reserved for things that will probably never happen, like taking a trip to the moon.

But writing? A wild dream? That's something to pay attention to.

I love her answer because I think she put into words what so many people feel. There is a real pull between exploring those things that make us come alive while, at the same time, being present to our responsibilities and our life stages. But why do we so often assume that pursuing those things we want to pursue can only be done at the expense of our responsibilities? Why can't we recognize and embrace the connection between the kind of art we long to make and the reality of our truest identity?

What if you desire to do a particular thing because God created you a particular way, not to tease you or to make you miserable, but to actually mold you into becoming more like him, for his glory and the benefit of others?

Could it be possible that the thing you most long for, the thing you notice and think about and wish you could do, is the thing you were actually made and are being equipped to do?

Could it also be possible that somewhere along the way you got the message that to follow desire would be selfish, when really, it would be the opposite?

Because I don't know when to keep my big nose out of other people's business, I asked this reader some of those questions. Her answer?

It could be possible.

One of the biggest obstacles we face when it comes to making art is our own idea about it. We make it too hard.

47

We make it so mysterious, so ethereal, so other-than us. We make it such a big deal. And it is, in a way.

But if you keep it there, it will continue to be too big to touch. You fear you'll wreck it all up if you dare to reach for it. So you leave it up there in the clouds, sparkling just out of reach. And it looks pretty and you cower beneath it as if it were something too important for you to handle. What do we call things that are placed up high, things we bow down low beneath?

We call them *idols*. And in a way I'm sure we don't intend, denying the art and the dream may be the very thing that opens the door to making the art the god rather than God himself. You revere and respect the artistic potential of a dream rather than recognizing God as the Creator who gives the gift of co-creation to us.

The woman who sent that email spoke of her desire to write, but as a writer myself, I would dare to say that it was about more than just *writing*. It was a desire to express herself fully *as* herself. And something deep within her sensed that writing played a part.

When I speak of desire, it isn't merely a desire to pursue a particular job, hobby, or vocation. I'm speaking of a desire running deeper than that. This is a longing for truth, for love, for God, and to honestly relate with others from the depths of who I most fully am.

Irenaeus of Lyons wrote this: "Life in man is the glory of God; the life of man is the vision of God." In other words, *the glory of God is a human being fully alive*. I wholeheartedly agree. The only problem is, too often human beings don't know what being fully alive actually means. And when we get a hint of it, instead of embracing it, we often run from it.

When was the last time you allowed yourself to consider who you are? I realize this is a personal question, requesting permission to access a part of your soul that is vulnerable and potentially unpredictable, much bigger than your capacity to control. And the idea of exposing that desire might be terrifying for you. But you aren't expected to face these depths alone.

In her book *Sacred Rhythms*, Ruth Haley Barton speaks of the importance of exposing our desires in the presence of Jesus.

> Jesus himself routinely asked people questions that helped them to get in touch with their desire and name it in his presence. He often brought focus and clarity to his interactions with those who were spiritually hungry by asking them, "What do you want? What do you want me to do for you?" Such questions had the power to elicit deeply honest reflection in the person to whom they were addressed, and opened the way for Christ to lead them into deeper levels of spiritual truth and healing.[3]

When I first began to realize I was falling in love with the man who is now my husband, I remember some deep and unexplainable feelings of guilt. There is no logical reason why I would have felt that way. I could analyze where those guilt feelings came from and why they may have been there. But the bottom line was I was terrified of my own desire.

Those same feelings of guilt and fear rose up again when I began to admit my deep desire to write, to express myself through the written word, and to do it in a way that encouraged others. The desire wasn't just about the writing. It was deeper, something hard to put into words. It had something to do with becoming more fully myself.

As I still sometimes struggle through the process of accepting the way I am made as a writer, an even deeper desire is becoming clear to me. I want to know Jesus and to live from him as the person, mother, and wife I uniquely am. I want to understand what it means to be fully alive as a woman whose life is united with the life of Christ. As it turns out, writing is part of that for me. It isn't the whole, but it is important.

Author Barbara Brown Taylor writes about a time in her life when she was desperate to discover what she was supposed to be doing with her life. She describes praying to God, asking him that very question in her book *An Altar in the World*.

God's answer to her was both surprising and infuriating. She sensed him saying this: *Do anything that pleases you, and belong to me.* This was her response:

> At one level, that answer was no help at all. The ball was back in my court again, where God had left me all kinds of room to lob it wherever I wanted. I could be a priest or a circus worker. God really did not care. At another level, I was so relieved that I sledded down the stairs that night. Whatever I decided to do for a living, it was not *what* I did but *how* I did it that mattered. God had suggested an overall purpose, but was not going to supply the particulars for me. If I wanted a life of meaning, then I was going to have to apply the purpose for myself.[4]

Does the idea of doing "anything that pleases you" sound completely other-than what you've grown up to believe is

God's will for your life? Does that feel as dangerous to you as it does to me? Maybe you are also aware of a stirring in your soul as you read those words, a waking up of desire that has been covered for too long. Does the Bible have anything to say about our desires as believers?

Desire Redeemed

Perhaps you're beginning to recognize some of the pursuits and passions that make you come alive. Your answers to those first-thought questions may help to shine some light on what those things might be.

But just because I have an experience of aliveness doesn't necessarily mean I should pursue that experience in all things.

Put me on a roller coaster and I've never felt more alive.

Hurt me and I can feel extremely alive in my anger or my bitterness, or my plans to get revenge. Driving fast makes me feel alive. So does a compliment. There are countless ways to feel alive, a lot of them illegal.

Pain has a way of tricking our souls into longing for relief more than anything else. Find relief? We call that life.

Our desire to feel alive can be twisted and corrupt, a feeling that can't be trusted. We arrive here upside down, clench-fisted, screaming for relief and warmth and safety, and we're not too picky about how we get it. What do we know of being alive? The heart of man is deceitful and desperately wicked. Isn't it?

For so long I was too afraid of my own mixed motives and false experiences of life to even consider waking up to my truest, most intimate desires. It felt wrong to want to uncover desire. But darkness and deceit is not all there is to the heart of a man or a woman. If we continue to live as though our hearts are desperately wicked, we have tragically misunderstood the work of Christ.

When God told Israel through the prophet Ezekiel he was planning to replace their heart of stone with a heart of flesh, he had us in mind. "And I will give you a new heart, and I will put a new spirit in you. I will take out your stony, stubborn heart and give you a tender, responsive heart. And I will put my Spirit in you so that you will follow my decrees and be careful to obey my regulations" (Ezek. 36:26–27).

What the NLT translates as "so that you will follow my decrees," the NIV says "move you to follow my decrees." He prophesies of a time when men and women will be moved on the inside toward God, when the law of God will no longer be on cold external stones but will be written on warm internal spirits.

That time is now. Jesus came down to us, lived a perfect life, and fulfilled the law of God, forever changing our relationship with the law so we don't have to look at it anymore. Now, we look to Jesus. He came so that you and I will be moved on the inside.

Bernard of Clairvaux describes this mysterious movement this way: "If you ask me how I know that the Lord is present, since His ways are past finding out, my answer is that the Word is living and active, and as soon as ever He entered me, He aroused my sleeping soul, and stirred and softened and pricked my heart, that had been sick and as hard as stone."

Now we are invited to move with the rhythm of his Spirit. The only way we can do that is because his *Spirit lives within us.*

What does this have to do with our desire to uncover our art?

Everything. Because now I have a new heart, a new purpose, a new *movement taking place within me*. As believers in the gospel, as partakers of the new covenant, as fellow sojourners on the road of the new way, maybe we don't have to be so suspicious of desire.

Pursuing desire is only toxic when we demand our desires be satisfied on our terms and in our timing. As recipients of the new heart of the Spirit, our deepest desire, when honestly realized, will always lead us to God.

In the Garden when God made man and woman in his image and then gave them a job to do, he left a lot of things unfinished. In Genesis 1:28 he tells them to "fill the earth and subdue it" (NIV). Timothy Keller wrote a book called *Every Good Endeavor* about connecting our work with God's work. He points out "the word 'subdue' indicates that, though all God had made was good, it was still to a great degree undeveloped. God left creation with deep untapped potential for cultivation that people were to unlock through their labor."[5] He left room for creativity, innovation, and personality. He left room in his creation for desire.

And so we continue to uncover what makes us come alive. We are not searching to find something we don't yet have, like treasure seekers with a map and a long journey ahead. Instead, we begin right where we are, like the tree planted firmly in place. We are not trying to become a better version of ourselves. Instead, we begin to uncover the person whom we have forgotten *we already are.*

Are you willing to honestly face where you currently are and will you refuse to edit desire as it surfaces in the present moment?

53

The Desire of Jesus

No matter how much I feel called to write about uncovering the art you were born to make and releasing the art you were made to live, it can't be ignored: the life of Christ was a one-way road to death. Without death, there is no spiritual life.

Did Jesus feel alive in the Garden while he asked God if there was any other way than the cross? Did he take delight in dying for us in a way that made him come alive? I consider the arrest of Jesus—his cross-carrying, his burden-bearing, his death.

And so we speak of desire, but how can we? Knowing the road Jesus walked and how it all played out, what does it matter what you really want to do?

As you begin to uncover hints of your own unique design and allow questions about your desires to rise to the surface, it may seem that discovering the shape of your own unique worship and then living as if you were truly alive feels a little too indulgent. But true desire doesn't search for escape or fame or adoration. *True desire is born out of death, of knowing I no longer live, but Christ lives in me.*

His desire was that all people might live. And the fulfillment of his desire was only realized through his death. Who am I to think that the road to realizing my own true desire would be paved with anything different? We often say things like, *Jesus died so I didn't have to,* but it's actually much worse.

The truth is, *Jesus died and so did I.*

But the worse morphs into better when we remember Jesus didn't stay dead. And neither do we. Let the dying moments remind us where to find the living.

Reading again the words used to describe how it feels when we are living life fully—awake, released, light, complete—my

54

mind keeps pushing me toward the word *resurrection*. How appropriate that living with our souls awake carries hints of the resurrection life. When we embrace our true design, we experience little tastes of the resurrection, of Jesus coming alive in us, of us coming alive within ourselves.

But new life is only possible when the old life dies. There is always death before resurrection. Remember the other things we feel when we honestly access the depths of our soul's desire—terror, unraveling, desperation. We look at the life of Jesus, his feet walking the one-way dusty road to death. He had to die before anything was resurrected. Mourning precedes morning; death comes before the dream. We long for the fullness of life, the freedom, the glory, and the joy. *But are we willing to embrace the death that must come first?*

We are all walking our own dusty roads. None of us are exempt from the prerequisites of a joyful release—death, surrender, brokenness, and humility. But the cross is beautiful because those heavy companions do not come alone. We do not have to bear their weight.

God left a love-trail through history, and it all points to the resurrection. And even though death precedes new life, love came first to pave the way. Love is the invisible hand of God made visible on the cross, in the tomb, through the resurrection.

And now his love is made visible through us, through the deepest desires of believers, through image bearers waking up in the presence of God.

I have felt death within myself as I've grasped for creativity or influence or joy. But I am learning how Christ's love-sacrifice of death replaces my longing for importance, and how his rising to new life sets me free from myself. I can dare to move into the world as the person I fully am because I am forgiven, empowered, and united with Christ in his death and his resurrection.

In a very real way, anything we do on earth that brings true joy or delight or fullfillment was made possible by death, by Love's sacrifice on a cross. Discovering what makes you come fully alive isn't the goal of life, but it is *evidence of life*. To be fully alive is impossible without the resurrection work of Christ.

Explore with abandon those things that make you come alive. If your flesh begins to put the art ahead of the Artist, disappointment will bring you back around again. If you begin to pursue lesser, secondary things, you need not fret so much about it. Trust that your clenching of second things will never fully satisfy.

Let disappointment do its deep work—remind you that your true desire is found, not in God's ways or God's will or God's blessings, but in God himself.

Once we are fully awake to the shape of our own souls, then perhaps we will be able to face desire no matter what we see there—to celebrate the joy of loving, grieve the loss of death, and release the art of our lives. We will more deeply know our Maker and what it means to reflect his glory as we carry his image into the world.

I realize there may still be a lot of questions. When you read how Barbara Brown Taylor asked God what she was supposed to do with her life and he answered, *Do whatever pleases you, and belong to me*, even if you can get over how dangerous that sounds, you may then be confronted with the next obvious frustration:

– I don't know what would please me. –

If you take the time to peer beneath the covers of fear and self-doubt and still don't have a clear sense of your own desire, one practice that might help to rescue the art that is alive within you is to spend a little time looking back.

4

rescue

Look Back

> She arrived with her own gifted form, with the
> shape of her own sacred soul. Biblical faith calls
> it the image of God in which we are all created.
>
> —Parker J. Palmer, *Let Your Life Speak*

Several years ago, I took one of those tests to find out
what kind of person I am—what jobs I would be good
at, what personality traits I have, what basically makes
me tick. Even though I was a grown-up person, I still longed
for someone else to tell me what I was supposed to be doing
with my life.

It's funny the things I sometimes do for affirmation. Those types of tests tell me everything I already know about myself. If the results show something different than what I believe to be true, I become suspect and question the validity of the test altogether. Even though I was the one who answered the questions. For myself. About myself.

Maybe you've done that too. Those tests don't challenge or move us to action. They simply state something that already is and give us some different ways to talk about it. They put what we say about ourselves into someone else's words. I love to be affirmed in things I already know.

The things that make us come alive are not news. They are not mind-boggling, shocking, I-never-would-have-thought-of-that things. In his book *Quitter*, Jon Acuff says we often take personality tests and think the results will be like showing up to our own surprise party. But no.

> More often than not, finding out what you love doing most is about recovering an old love or an inescapable truth that has been silenced for years, even decades. When you come to your dream job, your thing, it is rarely a first encounter. It's usually a reunion. So instead of setting out to discover this thing you love doing, you've got to change your thinking and set out to recover it, maybe even rescue it.[1]

Do we really need to wait for a test to tell us who we are? Do we need to fill out another set of questions about skill and talent and inclination? Those tests can be helpful and clarifying and often necessary. But don't forget the most basic test of all:

- Are you made in God's image?
- Were you woven together by God in the secret place?

- Do you have his loving, creative Spirit living inside you?
- Do you believe he wants to come out?

Good, then. So the next question is, how might he come out of you differently than he comes out of me? How are we to discover the shape of our souls? How do we get in touch with the fingerprint of the Divine on our lives?

Our passions aren't the goal, but they are signposts, like arrows pointing to our center. *Here is the path to the deepest part of who you are, how you are made, the poetry of your soul.*

In addition to looking within at desire as we did in the last chapter, it may also help to look back. As you do, pay attention to where hints of courage peek out from the folds of your life. Allow your first thoughts to rise to the surface without the pressure to make sense of them right now.

Remember When You First Ran Away

I sat at the old kitchen table my dad used as a desk in the basement corner, his black-and-white typewriter whispering invitation. Even at twelve, I knew the power of those keys. That typewriter held stories, more than I could tell in a lifetime. But I spent the summer of '89 chasing them down anyway.

I wrote of a creature named Milo who lived in the walls.

I wrote of magical flowers that never wilted.

I wrote of divorce, fear, fairies, and relationship.

In the fall of 1991 I sat midway to the back of Mrs. Smith's English class. Her gray curls were cropped short to her head and rimless glasses perched high up on her nose. Her calf-length skirt and sensible shoes painted her a nearly perfect portrait of an English teacher. She always wore a smile.

One afternoon when class was almost over, I sat waiting for her to hand back our term papers. I think mine was about ferrets. Or maybe Edna St. Vincent Millay.

She walked past my desk, placed my paper facedown in front of me, and continued passing out the rest. I turned it over and saw the A in the upper-left corner. Just beneath that, she wrote words of encouragement, the particulars of which I can't remember. But I know I took that paper home and showed my mom. I also know my mom stuck that paper to our fridge with two South Carolina–shaped magnets.

I always made good grades on essays.

In my early college days, I took an English class taught by a professor rumored to be the toughest in the department. He walked into class on the first day dressed in faded jeans, tennis shoes, and a rumpled sweater. His hair wild; his beard, unruly. He looked as though he had better things to do. The first gruff words out of his mouth were, "It is impossible to make an A in my class. The best among you will make a C. The rest of you will fail. That is, if you don't drop out first."

It was a dare.

I was thrilled.

The A I received in his class remains my most hard-earned one. He told me at the end of the year that if I ever needed a recommendation for anything, he would gladly give one. I never took him up on it.

I don't remember his name, but I remember his influence.

After receiving such encouraging feedback from eighth grade all the way into college on my writing, I did the most natural thing a young writer would do.

I chose to major in piano.

But since I didn't love piano enough to get better, I did the next natural thing a young writer would do. I dropped my piano major and began to study sign language interpreting. Naturally.

Actually, it makes more sense than you think.

The natural thing to do when hints of your own design scare you is to run.

Can you remember when you first ran away from this kind of desire, the kind carrying hints of your design?

This is what we do when we have forgotten who we are. We are desperately afraid of both our capacity for destruction as well as for beauty. We are terrified of our sin-burden as well as our image-bearing identity. We are suspicious of desire and don't trust our own ability to sort out first and second things.

Rescue Your Childhood Dreams

I used to fill notebooks with drawings of houses. Not house fronts, *house floor plans*. They were elaborate—front curvy staircases, secret passageways for the kids, special rooms just for dressing. They made no plumbing sense and were the stuff of fairy tales and English abbeys. One might look at that and think, *oh, well then, you clearly wanted to be an architect*.

No. I wanted to tell stories. I would stare at those floor plans for hours. If you watched me from across the room,

I may have looked like I was in a trance. But in my mind, elaborate drama was playing out. I made up stories for the invisible families who lived in my imaginary homes.

When I played Barbies as a girl, I *played Barbies*. I named each one and made up complicated relationship scenarios—every Ken had both a girlfriend and a bitter ex; Skipper was a babysitter, hired by a neurotic housewife with an addiction to shopping. I named each one—Gretchen, Bea, Dana, Ann—and they all had intricate and interwoven background stories. And if Grandma bought my sister and me the same doll? Evil twin bonus.

To my great disappointment, my sister didn't ever truly play Barbies. She set up their houses. She put their outfits together. She placed tiny plates and cups on their pink plastic tables and arranged their clothing stores. She would rarely, if ever, engage in conversation with my dolls or call them by the names I kept reminding her they had. It was as if she was in a different kind of fantasy world, one where I didn't know the language.

That trend continued even after she stopped "playing Barbies."

In high school, when other girls were hanging out with boys at football games, my sister would lock herself in her room and pull tiny purple flowers out of the books she dried them in. With Mom's blue Aqua Net hairspray, she would stick those stiff purple flowers to the frame of her door.

Squirt, stick.

Squirt, stick.

When she finished, she had an entire flower border around her door. It was free and lovely. Today she makes her living by writing for regular women who don't have a huge decorating budget, encouraging them to believe that *it doesn't have to be perfect to be beautiful*. But it started back in high school, with her squirting hairspray on flowers.

Rescue the Hope of Things to Come

My grandfather was a rather unhappy man in his living days. He stopped drinking only a few years before he died, yet he encouraged me in my writing as a young girl. I think he may have seen something in me he recognized in himself but couldn't quite touch. There were shadows of his design, whispers of his giftedness that I'm sure spoke to him in some way, but his demons drowned them out.

His son, my dad, is an alcoholic too. But he is living his story quite differently than my grandfather did. In the middle of his alcoholic days, my dad didn't go to church with us unless it was a holiday or special occasion. So when my mom, my sister, and I went to church, this is how he spent his Sunday mornings.

> When they leave for church, I open a beer, read the paper, and crank up the stereo. Sometimes with a few beers in me and the music loud, I stand and talk in a loud whisper. I catch myself acting like a teacher, talking and intellectualizing on things in the news, or politics, or sports, or music, or other things my mind randomly latches onto. Sometimes, in some foggy way, I see myself doing this explaining and persuading out in the future. Then I have another beer. I vacuum and wash the dishes so I don't feel totally useless. I take a nap. They come home from church. This becomes a normal Sunday morning.[2]

My alcoholic dad stood in the living room of that little white house on Gladstone Avenue and preached with a beer in his hand. He didn't know why and he couldn't explain it. *But it was in him to speak out.*

It didn't make sense.

At least, not at the time.

But looking back from where he now stands as a twenty-five-year-sober believer in Jesus? With a long career announcing on the radio? With years of experience as a teacher and mentor and a small group leader in churches?

Yes, now the actions of that confused alcoholic seem a little less confused and a lot more ordained.

His art was not something he came up with later in life once he got his act together. Hints of his art were coming out of him before he even understood it. Yours does that too.

God weaves his art into the very fiber of our being, so close that we can't not have at least some hint of it, even if we are drowning in addiction, blind to the truth, hardened by unforgiveness, paralyzed with fear.

Maybe you are drawn to the people and culture of another country but you can't explain why. Maybe you see the need for a ministry in your church or a particular job at your company that doesn't exist yet. You bring your camera to every wedding because you can't not take pictures of the bride. You write for free and it should feel like a waste, except that it doesn't and you don't have an answer for it. You stare at your living room and imagine ways to make it better, and then you do and it changes your mood.

It should be silly, except somehow to you, it isn't.

Maybe characters follow you around, waiting for a starring role in a story you haven't yet told. Not one of those characters are clear, but you are surrounded by a smoky cloud of faceless witnesses; the fog is thick with story but you can't see a thing. And so you wait. It isn't time to tell their stories. It may never be time. But it's important for you to embrace your desire to tell them.

Sometimes inspiration toward that thing that makes you come alive follows after you so hard and so loud that you look around to see how everyone else is reacting to this most obvious explosion of creativity happening right here in this room. It is bright and tangible and full. But other times, it speaks of future, not-yet things to come. It whispers for you to prepare so that it isn't so surprising when the story shows up one day, demanding you to tell it or to live it, ready or not. The Spirit of the living, loving God speaks into our lives and offers us shadows of things to come, blurry and unclear. But no less real.

And so when you hear the whispers, *One day, there will be fiction. Children. Teaching. Building. Travel. Love. Writing . . .* don't ignore them. It doesn't mean that things will turn out exactly as you think. They won't. But I do believe God fully provides for us in the present while at the same time faintly hints about the future. And sometimes, as he moves in us and around us in the moments of our day, he nudges us in whispers and desire toward something he has for us later.

It's why an alcoholic who isn't even a believer can stand in a room and pretend to teach and not know why. It's not because he had an idea that he would like to try that out one day. *It's because teaching was woven into the fiber of his being when he was knit together in his mother's womb.*

We—a people with a full capacity to love and learn and create and live—we did not just happen. We were *made* by design, held together by a Person.

We don't have to be so afraid of desire. It's time instead to wake up to it. In the waking, maybe we will begin to see that instead of principles to follow, life is more like a rhythm to move with.

Your childhood dream delights God. I don't say that because every secret dream will come true. But *having* a dream is evidence of a person who is fully alive. Having a dream is a reflection of the image of God.

In a class I took taught by author and psychologist Dr. Larry Crabb, he said this about hope: "We are sustained not by what we see happen but by what we *know* will happen."

In the Old Testament, the prophets encouraged the people to look forward to the day of the Lord. They never saw that day, but they hoped for it. God told Abraham his descendants would outnumber the stars. Abraham never lived to see that dream realized, but he lived with the hope of its future fulfillment. God's people hoped for a coming Messiah. The disciples hoped for the gospel to spread. We now hope for the return of Christ to reestablish his reign on earth.

Hope is powerful and important.

My husband, John, has a friend who, for lack of a better way of saying it, helps him think. Jerome listens to John and helps to cast vision for his life. He asks him a lot of questions about his desires and dreams for the future.

John's time with Jerome is life-giving and encouraging. When I asked him why that time is so important to him, he said this: "Because when he asks about my desires and dreams and takes them seriously, it means he believes I am a person worth dreaming with."

He didn't say anything about those desires or dreams being realized. He said there is value in exploring desire and having someone listen.

Immediately, I remembered my recent visit to the Philippines with Compassion International, an organization dedicated to releasing children from poverty in Jesus' name. Sitting in the small, cluttered office in the capital city of Manila, one of the volunteers with Compassion explained how, from the time they are twelve, every child registered in the program begins to build a book called "My Plan for Tomorrow."[3]

Every year they write down what they dream to become and plans for how to get there. The children consider four simple areas of life and come up with actionable objectives for each of those areas. I flipped through one of these journals as the Compassion volunteer spoke to our team. I will never forget what I saw there on the page, written in a child's handwriting:

> To *have zero waste river.*
> To *finish my study.*
> To *have higher height.*

When you encourage kids living in poverty to put dreams like this into words, it implies you believe their life is worth dreaming over and they have a tomorrow worth living for.

It doesn't matter if you are a Filipino child living in poverty or a grown man in the United States living with plenty. We are all made to desire something for our future.

There is a mysterious connection between having hopes for our future and being secure in our identity now. This doesn't mean every child's dream for "higher height" will come true. But it's still important for them to have those dreams.

Exploring desire might be uncomfortable for you. In one way, it almost seems cruel to ask you to access this part of your soul, because really, on earth, there can never be complete satisfaction of our deepest desires. To imply that there can be is unfair and untrue. But hope does not disappoint. When we recognize the place where our desire runs parallel to that of Christ's, then we will live in the midst of the now-but-not-quite-yet with a peace that goes beyond our ability to understand.

When we rescue the dreams of our childhood and respect the hope of things to come, we are agreeing with the Trinity: *I am an image bearer. I have a job to do.*

We trust he knew what he was doing when he made us as we are. We accept ourselves because of the work of Christ, and we accept his invitation to us to enter the world as co-creators with him.

Sarah Masen reflected something I couldn't hold on to but knew was true. Her art stirred up a thirst within me for more of something I couldn't define. She was, as C. S. Lewis put so eloquently, "the scent of a flower we have not found, the echo of a tune we have not heard, news from a country we have never yet visited."[4]

She shared a glimpse of the glory of God and it left me wanting more. Not just more of the art she was making, but it stirred up a longing in me to make art myself, to reflect the glory of God in ways only I can, and to move into the world as the *poiema* he made me to be.

And so we continue the uncovering.

If you have a clearer idea of the shape of your soul and the design God had in mind when he made you, beware the temptation to take what you know and run in your own strength.

As you look within to consider your deepest desires and look back to remember the desires you once had, the only safe place to move forward with them is into the presence of God. Where do our feet now stand? Where is our surest foundation?

I know the fatigue that may come with introspection, with looking within and looking back. There is only one place to go when our hands are filled with dreams and desire. It's time to sink into God.

5

sink

Look Up

Remember—the root word of humble and human is the same: humus: earth. We are dust. We are created; it is God who made us and not we ourselves. But we were made to be co-creators with our maker.[1]

—Madeleine L'Engle, *Walking on Water*

I stand in clear water at the edge of the world where the Carolina coast shakes hands with foreign friends— *Hello, Africa. Hello, Europe. Hello, drops that carried our ancestors over and salted the fish on my plate last night.*

I play a little game, warm water up to my waist. *How long can I keep my feet in one place?* The sea is subtle today, confident enough in her power to take a break from showing off. Her waves are gentle, rhythmic, tame.

I lock my knees, set my eyes on the gray outline of a shrimp boat, pour all my power into keeping my feet firmly planted. But even these training-wheel waves move me. I spread my hands upon the water, hold out arms, dig in heels. I've yet to meet the person who can challenge the sea in any kind of game and win.

The sea smiles. She breathes. I lose my balance.

Finally, I declare defeat. I loosen my knees and surrender my body to the unforced swaying of the sea. My twin girls hold each other's hands far to my left. I can hear them laughing, faces turned out to the line of blue on blue.

The sea speaks a mysterious language, one the dolphins and the coral respect more than I do. The sea has rhythm and motion, chaos and calm. She is untamable, independent, strong. *And yet.*

There is One who tells her where her proud waves halt. You can point to her limits, her boundaries. There is a line where wet sand meets dry, and the line is wavy and it changes with the tides.

But there is a line and God draws it with his finger.

We want to live a beautiful life that means something. We want to create and love and move on purpose. We want to make art. We know we are image bearers and our hands itch for the job we were made to do. But we cannot push results ahead of receiving. We cannot dig in our heels against the natural rhythm of the sea and expect to win, stretch out stiff arms in the face of God and refuse to receive what he has to offer.

Follow the Gaze of Jesus

The sea can tell us more than our lists ever will about how to live life as the poem of God. Once we have an idea of the art that is alive deep within us, we then begin to move to the rhythm of the Spirit of God. But how does the Spirit of God move?

Let's peer into the past, into the Upper Room in John 13. It's suppertime and Jesus sits with his disciples around the table.[2] He knows his hour has come. He fills the basin with water, wrings out the towel. Dirt gathers at the bottom, dirty water swishing over the side. Jesus, the Son who does only what he sees his Father doing, who reveals his Father's glory in everything he does, kneels down before men and washes their feet.

These men will turn their backs on him when things get dark and one man will betray him altogether. Still, he moves silently among them, offering no explanation or description. Immanuel, God with us.

The air is awkward with silence. No one quite knows what to say. This foot washing is uncomfortable and unprecedented. Who ever heard of a master serving the servants?

Peter is up next.

These other men, his brothers and fellow disciples, they have no sense. They let Jesus do the work of a servant. Not so with Peter. He knows who Jesus is. "Lord, do you wash my feet?"

73

"You don't understand now, Peter. But you will."

"Never shall you wash my feet!"

"If I do not wash you, you have no part with me."

Peter, all enthusiasm, all religious commitment, all proud activity. "Lord, then wash not only my feet, but also my hands and my head."

Peter has a glimpse of how he might be useful to God, and something wakes up within him. *This is what I'm here for, Lord. I'm all in.* He seems to want to please God, but he's missing the point.

The towel sinks down into the water, dirt collected from the feet of other disciples swirling around, brown and gray. Jesus looks up, meets dark eyes, takes in a calm breath.

"You already bathed before the meal. Only the feet are necessary."

Can Peter possibly know the depths of his own sin? The ugliness that lurks beneath all his good intentions? Does he not see the dipping of the towel, the movement of the hands, the rubbing clean of dirty feet? Is he not aware of this rhythm and movement of the Son in his presence? Peter's enthusiasm to be washed all over draws twisted attention to his pride and self-dependence. He teaches me what not to do—when something begins to come alive within me, when I begin to sense an area where I might be able to offer something to God, I would be wise to first consider what Jesus is offering me. There is a place to shut the mouth, still the hands, and receive what Immanuel offers.

Jesus always looks into the eyes of his Father, moving only when his Father says to move. To live in the rhythm of God is to allow Jesus to do what he sees his Father doing even when it doesn't make sense to me. Don't let me add to it. Don't let me try to help. Don't let me draw attention to myself.

Let me first stretch out my dirty feet and receive the gift.

With clean feet and wide eyes, the disciples lean in and listen to Jesus.

"If I then, the Lord and the Teacher, washed your feet, you also ought to wash one another's feet. For I gave you an example that you also should do as I did to you."[3]

Maybe this means we should have regular foot washings, make sign-up sheets for whose turn it is with the towel. Don't forget to paint your toenails, it's foot-washing day at church.

Or maybe it means something more. Maybe Jesus is inviting them into a relationship of *do as I do* rather than pointing them to a list and saying, *Copy me.*

What is this rhythm? How did Jesus move and live on earth? Jesus did as he saw his Father do, in the energy and by the direction of his Father, then moved toward his disciples in humility.

And he says to his disciples, "Do as I did to you."

That day, it was to wash their feet.

How is he moving *this* day? Now the Spirit of Jesus lives inside me. He intends to continue moving on earth in me the way he moved on earth as himself—doing only what he sees his Father doing. What does this mean for us?

In the words of author and Bible teacher J. E. Conant:

> This spiritual life is not native to us, nor can it be *developed* out of anything we have or are by nature. It must be *given* to us. So God has given us eternal life, "and this life is in His Son," through whose possession of us when we believed on him we were born from above. . . .

The life of a Christian, therefore, is the life of Christ within us through the Holy Spirit. It is not a life similar to his, it is *his life*.[4]

As we continue to uncover the shape of our unique design, we need not feel the pressure to figure out what to do with it. When he told Jesus to wash his whole body, it seems as if Peter believed he had something to offer, on his own and by himself. But Christ, who was in his very nature God, gave up the right to do anything on earth by himself. He only did what he saw his Father do.

Jesus encouraged his disciples toward this simple truth— *I do as I see my Father do. Now you do the same as you depend, not on your skill, your talent, your ability, or your timing, but on me.*

After washing their feet, Jesus speaks words of comfort, telling them not to let their hearts be troubled, to believe in God and also in him. And then, he says this: "If I go and prepare a place for you, I will come again and receive you to Myself, that where I am, there you may be also. And you know the way where I am going."[5]

Jesus does what he sees his Father do, turns around and does it for these men, then promises his Spirit so they can do it for one another.

Receive, respond, repeat.

But words meant to comfort seem instead to confuse. Thomas speaks up, says out loud what perhaps the others are thinking. "Lord, we do not know where You are going, how do we know the way?" Thomas wants a road map, a list, indisputable directions.

Jesus answers him directly. "I am the way, and the truth, and the life; no one comes to the Father but through me."

There is only one way, one truth, and one life. One way for the many of us. One divine nature reflected through the lives of millions of image bearers.

God comes down to come in. And then? He comes out in a million little ways.

We might want to point to the act he did. Now we should wash feet! That's it. That's the one way to be a believer on earth! But maybe he was showing us something deeper, something of looking up to the Father, then moving in faith; something of serving with a whole heart even when it doesn't make sense to anyone. Something of love in the face of our enemies.

Foot washing is the way, the truth, and the life?

No. He says, I AM the way.

And sometimes I AM washes feet.

Why Sinking Is the Only Way to Float

I flip to one of my favorite verses, Psalm 46:10. "Cease striving and know that I am God" (NASB). The word we read as *cease* is sometimes read *be still*, *let go*, *return*. But the first way, the original way, is a verb that means *sink*.

Sink and know that I am God.

As I begin to wake up to the art that is alive within me, sinking seems counterintuitive. *No! I'm supposed to float! Isn't that why we've been uncovering my passion and desire? So I can succeed in life?* My flesh tells me I don't want to sink. I don't even like getting my hair wet. Fear and logic tell me I need to stay in the boat to make things happen, not step out into the water and risk drowning. But my spirit knows there is something sacred in this sinking, something I want to know more about.

The God who divided water from land in the beginning, who told water to rise up like wall-towers for Moses, who bosses the sea and walks on top of it toward his disciples, who dipped a towel into dirty water and washed the dirty feet of men in the Upper Room, this God tells his people to sink.

Not float or kick or figure out a way to make a raft. Not learn to swim or doggie-paddle to the nearest shore.

Sink.

Even deeper, even more offensive, even worse?

The short definition of this Hebrew word *raphah* is "fail."[6]

Fail and know that I am God.

As we begin to uncover the art God had in mind when he made us, as we begin to wake up to our deepest desires and expose them in the presence of Jesus, there is a real possibility we will become overwhelmed with one of two realities in front of us. Either we have lived a lot of our lives denying who we truly are and we feel discouraged for the wasted time, or we see what we most deeply desire and want to forsake everything in order to have those desires satisfied now.

We are in danger of sinking into either regret and anxiety or self-effort and self-expression.

But God invites us into a different kind of sinking.

This isn't just a sinking or a falling into death. This isn't a flailing-backward-off-a-building kind of falling, a sinking into the frigid depths of an impersonal sea. This kind of sinking is one into *knowing*, knowing he is God.

Without looking up to God, sinking leads to drowning. But when my eyes are locked on his, sinking tells a different story.

Drop the hands and let the knees be weak. Loosen the grip and let the arms open wide. Bow the head and let the eyes close tight. We cannot do this life. We cannot parent these children. We cannot lead this company. We cannot change this world. We cannot make this art.

Not alone. Not on our own. Not without sinking first.

In the act of sinking into God, of looking up at him from the depths of our own inadequacy, we begin to know who he is. In turn, we know who we are as well.

When Looking to God Doesn't Feel Like Enough

It will get messy. We don't show up in the world with our bag filled with skill and talent and look around to see where we might come in handy. We don't look within us at desire and then back at our childhood dreams and set off with our newly realized abilities and move into the world in our own strength.

We'll show up and trip through the loving, spill the basin of dirty water, turn our noses up at ugly toes. We'll plunge our hands in up to our elbows, sometimes with a rotten mood, a broken heart, an ulterior motive. We can't wait until we're ready to love before we start loving, before we start carrying God's image into the world. We already are the poem of God. Nothing we do can change that. But in the midst of a filled-up life, it can be easy to forget.

I stand at the top of the John Hancock building in Chicago, stare down at the toy cars moving along Lake Shore Drive. From up high, it looks like a Lego city with Matchbox cars driving next to a pretend lake of bathtub water. There's a

Barbie swimming pool on the top of a Lego building and I stand here knowing it's real but feeling oddly like a giant person.

I'm Godzilla and the city is pretend and any moment I will take a step and squash it all. Watch me lift my foot! But when I do, I lose my balance and step far away from the window because I'm not Godzilla and the building I stand in is real and I took the forty-five-second elevator ride to the top that proves it.

The city takes my breath away. I know it's all concrete and right angles and gray and brown and processed. But maybe that's the amazing part in a way. *People* made this, made these buildings to touch the sky. And here I stand, in midair, looking down at all those cars holding all those people with all their stories and jobs and lists.

I marvel at my fascination with the whole city experience. I'm an introvert wearing extroverted skin. I smile here, feel the pulse, settle into the pace. I come alive with the movement, the lights, the color. I am big and important and things are happening. Opportunities feel touchable here.

But possibility can talk the ears off a billy goat, so after a few days, I want to crawl under the bed and hide. I want to cradle my head in my hands and find a quiet so deep I feel it all the way down to my bones.

An artful life isn't always an easy thing to embrace, even in the best of circumstances. In the sharp cold of midwinter two weeks after our family trip to Chicago, John and I head to the coast alone. We stand by the sea, heads weary from the travel, hands open with time to spare, and we don't have much to say. It is lovely. Still, I feel pressure to make the most out of our time. My life is the city but my soul is the sea and I can't figure out how to make them get along. I am aware of the to-do list I made on the plane. It takes a full day to shake it. And even then, it's a fight. *I have a disease*, I think to myself. *I am addicted to measurable productivity.*

I am bound to my own usefulness, bigheaded with my own accomplishments, crushed by my shortcomings. I am capable of making beautiful art, but I am also capable of turning the art into something it was never meant to be. I miss the presence of Jesus in my current moments. I miss the soul breath. I miss the smallness, the doorway through which I must walk to find freedom from the ever-moving treadmill of life.

Even if I steal time to find the sitter, pack the bags, pay the money, sit through the layovers, and fly to the shore to relax, sometimes once I get there I forget to step off the treadmill. And I realize as I tap my foot on sand that I have forgotten my truest identity. I am a poem, but I live tethered to my programs.

I wake the next morning, walk out to the coast, and stand alone, boots on sand as fine as sugar, winter wind whipping straight through the quiet. I'm not Godzilla now; instead I'm microscopic. I stand at the edge of the world and wonder how anyone who comes to this coast could ever leave. I want to fill my soul up with beauty enough to last a week, find that water blue on a paint chip at Lowe's, and color the world *Sea*.

How could I have ever felt alive in the city when there's this? I am sand-small tiny, in awe of this beauty. I feel myself relax with the pace of this place.

Uncovering the art feels like that sometimes. At first you want to point to it and headline it and say, *This! This is what I was made for!* And you delight in the big-city experience of discovery and movement. But soon, you begin to want appreciation and attention for your efforts, billboards to light up your plans, more time to work all hours of the night in the city that never sleeps. Before you realize what has happened, you're looking at you more than looking at God and you start to sink into self-effort and expectation. But being an image bearer is about reflecting God as a human, not about becoming a god myself.

Small is fast becoming my new home. Sometimes it hurts to be small. We work so hard to be big, and sometimes we catch a glimpse of it. If they don't see how big we are? Then we must become bigger. We think we have many rights and we hold them with both hands.

But Jesus came down. Became poor. Became less. Became small. He surrendered his rights to do life on his own, looking to his Father before he made a move.

I read the words of my friend and singer/songwriter Shaun Groves as he honestly struggles with this question—in our pursuit of our art and our vocations, do we insist on more, bigger, higher, up?

> From more to less. Served to service. From honor to degradation. From eternal to time-bound. God to flesh. Heaven to earth.
>
> Is it possible that the descending way of Jesus might be God's way for me?
>
> I'm thankful for the Josephs who govern from Pharaoh's side for the good of the masses, for the Esthers who influence the influencers and change the trajectory of history.

But where are those people called by God to step down, leave behind, earn less, influence fewer, to follow? Does God only call His Son to downward mobility? Or does God call me downward too and I fail to recognize His voice because it sounds too backward?

Forward or backward. Up or down. More or less. Follow.[7]

Shaun Groves, "Downward Mobility"

The small only get that way because they first recognize how big they thought they were. I can handle this life. I can make things happen. I must!

A few disappointments later, we realize we cannot make this life work. We sink heavy into our own smallness and it's in that place where we lose our life. And also find it.

The Relief of Not Having What It Takes

We, each of us, have our reasons why we don't have what it takes to make art, to be who we really are. We list out our reasons like a script and playact our way through life as little less-thans. But there is a difference between embracing your smallness in the presence of Christ and feeling like a nobody in the presence of others.

Maybe you feel guilty for having a passion without a job description or are waiting for permission to be qualified. Maybe you know you have a few things you're good at, but you don't see their value in the scope of "things that *really* matter." All of this reeks of self-focus.

Let me speed up the process.

You don't have what it takes.

And neither do I.

The upside-down mystery of God is that you can still be a miracle gift even when you have no idea where your giftedness comes from, even when all you can bear to do is know you are loved and live like it's true. You are art and you make art, but you are not your art. You are God's art. As you continue to embrace the Spirit of Christ in you, as you continue to bend your ear toward the deep desires of your heart, trust that God is intuitive enough to move in and through you no matter your fear or insecurity.

> We are always on stage. We are always in a novel, and even when no other characters are around, the art continues. The Triune audience watches. You have been given your body. You have been given your ancestors, your natural strengths and your natural weaknesses. The back-story is all in place. You have been drawn, described, and placed on a stage un-like any other—the Globe. And you have been given your freedom to act.[8]
>
> N. D. Wilson, *Notes from the Tilt-A-Whirl*

We are made in the image of God and are being remade inside the person of Jesus Christ. He holds all things together even when it looks like they're falling apart. His grace fills in my lack.

Our dark-haired daughter is our firstborn (by three minutes) and we put Grace in her name, right in the middle. It's a word I spent many years circling around, with eyes narrowed and arms crossed, a word I thought I understood. But that was back when I knew everything.

This grace is higher, wider, deeper, stronger, and other-than me. We put grace up on our two-pan balance scale and try to come up with something that will be equal to it on the other side. But like the ocean, grace wins every time, stays heavy on the right, sinks hard into the middle of my good intentions and mixed motives.

Since it's part of her name, I think of grace every time I call her. Every time she lags behind, skins her knee, shouts at her brother, reads me her book, runs to the neighbor's house—every place she is, *there is grace*. It fits there in the middle. It floats around her as she plays. I pray she grows to know that, even though she will never fully understand what her name means, she will also never be able to escape it.

Neither will I. Neither will you.

What if you began to see your art as something other than your idea? What if it was less lofty and more necessary to your daily rhythm? What if your art is part of a bigger picture, part of a daily grace God has in mind for someone else?

We are all Peter, standing ankle deep in cold water. The Lord walks toward us, the arm of God stretched strong in our direction. We lock eyes and feel the invitation to hold his gaze.

There is nothing about his appearance that should draw us, yet we are pulled into the fullness of heaven reflected in his dark eyes. The chaos around us rages and swirls. There is no way this water will hold.

Aren't we all scared fishermen in a boat, the sea raging all around us, the darkness closing in? Don't we all grasp for our nets and long to catch our fish because *this is our job*, *this is our passion!* But the sea just won't cooperate.

You think living your art is too hard in this chaos. You need to calm this storm to survive. The first things of God seem too much to ask. Trust? Believe? Embrace my image-bearing identity no matter my fear and insecurity? No way. Give me a boat. Throw me a life vest, I can't handle the waves. I am falling into second things and I can't find a way out.

There is a time to sink down into the depths, to see the hopelessness of my life without God. Sink, fail, and know God, because the invisible world of heaven doesn't play by our rules. And so as Peter, I have to first know the depths of my own ugliness before I will be willing to stay my gaze on Christ. If I think, even for a moment, that I can handle these waves on my own, I will drop down heavy into the darkness of the water.

Believe in myself and I sink into the waves of worry, procrastination, daily tasks, and diagnoses. There is no dry ground in sight.

But sink hard into God and he will buoy the soul on top of the water.

Stepping out of the boat and walking toward Jesus, I realize how looking deep into the eyes of God is art all by itself.

Dying is our invitation to live.

Down is the only way up.

So Peter went over the side of the boat and walked on the water toward Jesus. But when he saw the strong wind and the waves, he was terrified and began to sink. "Save me, Lord!" he shouted.

Jesus immediately reached out and grabbed him. "You have so little faith," Jesus said. "Why did you doubt me?" (Matt. 14:29–31)

Upon this rock he builds his church. Peter of little faith, who stares at the waves and lets the waves overcome him,

Peter who refuses to receive the service of Jesus in humility, Peter who suggests that the Lord could avoid the cross—he is called a rock and given the keys to the kingdom of heaven. The miracle, upside-down work of God is that our failure isn't an obstacle, it's an *opportunity* to remember to sink into God. Not having what it takes is not a liability, *it's a prerequisite*. Maybe there is hope for us after all.

I look hard at the place where I stand and realize it isn't the kind of certainty I expected. I'm looking for dry ground, but God gives me water and tells me to sink. But this is not a sinking into worry or self-help. This is a sacred sinking into knowing he is God.

6

see

Look Around

No one is ever united with Jesus Christ until he is willing to relinquish not sin only, but his whole way of looking at things. To be born from above of the Spirit of God means that we must let go before we lay hold, and in the first stages it is the relinquishing of all pretense. What our Lord wants us to present to him is not goodness, nor honesty, nor endeavor, but real, solid sin; that is all he can take from us. And what does he give in exchange for our sin? Real, solid righteousness.[1]

—Oswald Chambers

As you begin to open yourself up to the desires buried deep within you and as you become more aware of those moments when you feel most alive, there will be critics. And they will be loud.

see

The more you uncover, the louder they'll get.

Criticism is key in the artist's life. How we handle our critics could be the difference between creating art that matters and allowing the art to die.

Our critics come in all different shapes. It could be anyone from the anonymous writer of a hateful email, to a loving and generous mentor. Some critics will want to kill your art, while others are honestly trying to help you make it better.

While the critique from the hateful critic hurts, most of us don't have to deal with horribly hateful critics on a daily basis. On the other hand, it may be hard for us to accept critique even when it comes from someone who has our best work and our best interest in mind. You might react to your critics differently depending on your stage of life, your age, your gender, or even your personality. Some of my own ideas about criticism are still evolving with each experience. Maybe they always will be.

While we'll take a brief look at the shape our critics might take, I'm going to focus primarily on our artistic response to the critic. No matter if a critic intends to be hurtful or helpful, I've found in my own life that I have to handle all types of criticism in the same way: remember who I am, remember who God is, and remember not to take my work too seriously.

You need not have people always agree with you, but the critiques to most seriously consider are the ones coming from those who *believe* in you. If someone who believes in you, your work, your art, and your passion is disagreeing with you or pointing out a weakness or a way to make things better, it is helpful and healthy to consider their words with humility

89

and grace. Resist the urge to close yourself off from them. Instead, open yourself in the presence of Christ and allow Christ's words to partner with the critique in order to show you the truth.

But if the critic not only disagrees with you but also doesn't believe in you, their words may be more difficult to sort out. But we can't just say, "Ignore the harsh and hateful critic!" because that isn't always wise or possible. Many of us live, day in and day out, with what to us are harsh critics in our lives. We have to hear their critique of us on a daily basis, including the resident critic who lives inside our own heads. It isn't as easy as just deciding not to pay attention. We can't close our eyes and hope they'll go away. We have to be willing to see them and decide what to do with their words.

See the Shape Your Critic Takes

My fear of the critics sometimes keeps me up at night. They sit at the foot of my bed snacking on crackers and dropping their crumbs in my sheets. I can't even brush the grit away because I'm too obsessed with listening to their crunching. *What will they eat next? How will they choose to criticize me?*

They don't take the time to look me in the eye. They look past me, beyond me to something more important. Other critics, maybe? They have no regard for the way my eyebrows furrow and my hands wring. They don't see me falling apart.

These imaginary critics are sophisticated and rotten. They are scholarly and sensible. They sigh with indifference, check their nails, pick the lint off their slick, black pants. Sometimes they wear hats.

All artists struggle with the voice of the critics. The reviewers who hoard their stars, sit on their thumbs, write their critiques without a hint of humanity.

You say I'm being a baby.

You're right.

You listen to me now, but then you shake your head, pity me, tell me it's a privilege to be in a position where people care enough about what I have to say to critique it in the first place.

You are right about that too.

And then you begin to gather your things, dig around in your bag for your keys, because our conversation is over. *It's been great chatting with you, Emily, but I'm not a writer, so I don't really have critics like that.*

Really?

You make a different kind of art and your critics show up wearing different kinds of hats, but they still show up.

You do the art of a teacher, and today the principal sits in the back of the room with her pen and her bored expression.

You do the art of a pastor, and today you read a letter from a man who sings in the choir. He is not happy with you.

You do the art of a mother, and today you broke the jelly jar and forgot to take the brownies to the PTA. Your seven-year-old hears you cuss. You imagine what the other moms will think of you.

You do the art of a doctor, and today you have a meeting with a woman who disagrees with your diagnosis. Her husband is dead. She brings her lawyer.

We work hard to avoid critique. We think the answer is to get rid of the critic and get on with our lives. If that pesky person would just move or disappear or transfer or quit, we could remain unbothered and uninterrupted. We could make such beautiful art!

Are we willing to take an honest look around at those people who seem to stand in the way of our attempts at making art? Are we willing to admit how we might be putting them in a position reserved for God alone? Are we willing to see things differently?

See the Real Reason the Critique Hurts

We sit in her small office and she waits for me to speak. Instead I begin to cry. I am embarrassed, wishing I could keep it together. I apologize once, twice. She merely listens and hands me a tissue.

We begin to talk about where the tears come from and here they come again. I instinctively repeat my apology and then shake my head at my own mess.

She speaks then, tilts her head to one side. "Do you have any words besides 'I'm sorry' to describe your tears?"

As it turns out, I do.

The imaginary critics have hit me hard recently. It's difficult to trust God, it feels awkward to be who I most deeply am, and it seems like the eyes of an invisible audience are trained in my direction, waiting for me to make a fool of myself.

I'm here in her office to talk about my fear of hateful criticism, but if I were to stop crying and speak from a place of courage, I would have to confront the truth about the tears.

The truth is, I'm apologizing for things I know aren't sin to avoid acknowledging the things that are. It's easy to say, "I'm so sorry I'm crying," because I know crying isn't wrong. It's harder to say, "I'm crying to avoid talking about what is really going on inside my desperate soul."

So what is really going on? It's the question you have to ask yourself when the words of the critic sting. Look further down than you've looked before until you get to the most basic level of your pain. For me, it's this: Even after all the growing up I've done, I want to please man more than I want to trust God. The bottom line is, I am a glory hog. I don't want to reflect the image of God, I want to embody it. And that is why I fear the critics. It's because they say out loud what I most fear in my heart. They remind me that I am not God after all.

What if, instead of brushing our emotions aside and apologizing for the brokenness, we decided to go further beneath our immediate hurt and discover what's going on inside? What if we really believed that Jesus is present when people are broken, and the way he chooses to move and comfort will often be through the lives of fellow believers, journeying image bearers, living their broken lives with us?

What if I began to believe that the critique isn't just an unwelcome part of the art-making process but might actually make the art better?

See the Gifts Only a Critic Can Bring

The automatic doors on the minivan quit working right around spring break. I pull the door closed and walk inside to do the dishes, only to discover the sink has clogged and the water won't go down. My favorite leggings have a hole, but I wear them anyway because every other option is dirty. I sit to do work, and as soon as I meet one deadline, three more show up in my inbox.

On this already bad day, the critics show up louder, stronger, and more annoying than ever before.

He says a word that is dismissive.

I feel like an idiot in her presence.

They had an expectation that I failed to meet.

Again.

We are offended when we are hurt. We are offended when they misunderstand. We are offended when they don't acknowledge our feelings. We are only offended because we forget we have died.

If there's one thing certain to change your life, it's death. "For you died to this life, and your real life is hidden with Christ in God" (Col. 3:3).

We live false lives when we hold on to the old life and refuse to acknowledge our death. If we grasp the threads of our comfortable lives, second things—like praise from critics—become first things.

And so when we are hurt, we think we have a right to our offenses.

Except we don't.

Death doesn't always look like a tragedy. Sometimes death is a slowly dripping faucet. A word, a look, a disapproval. And even though these things can't be compared to real danger or true poverty, disappointment and weariness can drip the life right out. Slow. Quiet. Drip.

I talk to myself with my critical hat on. It is black and has a feather and critical Emily knows everything. She knows why I am an idiot. She's memorized my weaknesses, and recites them at all the worst times. She makes a little rhyme and puts them in a song and that nasty tune weaves its sticky melody through every corner of hope in my heart.

The critic in our head is hard to confront, mainly because we tend to believe every ugly word she says. Her mantra just becomes part of our normal, like how we always part our hair on the same side or keep our food from touching on our plate. It's just how things are.

Our internal critics shift in the shadows of our minds, difficult to capture and, therefore, reject. Our external critics, on the other hand, are harder to ignore. My immediate and natural response is embarrassment: *Somebody doesn't like what I'm doing and now everyone knows*. At least when I'm my own critic, I can keep my weakness a secret. But have someone point it out in public and I feel like giving up for good.

For that very reason, I'm learning it's somewhat easier to deal with the external critic than it is to contend with the ones in our heads. Sure, they pass us notes and send us emails and confront us at the worst times. But something happens when the critic speaks up, something that perhaps can't happen any other way.

When the external critic speaks—dismissing our art, narrowing eyes at our carefully thought-through choices, misunderstanding our intent, pointing out a weakness—he reminds us of all the reasons we were afraid to move in the first place. And for a bit, we are paralyzed by fear of ever moving again. One wrong move, and they could start pointing.

It isn't a thicker skin that I need. The words of the critic might sting, even if they are well-intended. The sting means I am alive and I am human. I wish I were stronger, tougher, more naturally resilient. But the critical voice is teaching me my humanity, *and that is not a bad thing.*

There, in the clenched hand of the critic is a gift he may not realize he's giving you, one you don't recognize at first. But there it is, the gift of your own smallness, your own *Yes, I am a mess. Yes, I want your approval and agreement. Yes, I want to be loved and admired. Yes, I want to be right.* The critic's words point out my insecurities—but in seeing those, he shows me myself.

When I finally see myself, I can be laid open before God. In the opening, I see the root of this desire for approval is less about the critic and more about me. I showed up on the scene of the world crying and clenching and needing salvation. So did you. So did your critic. But it isn't the critic's fault I am desperate for worth and security and approval and permission.

This is the shape I was born into, the curve of my flesh, the crookedness of my own heart, the twisted desire to be enough on my own and by myself.

My critics don't cause that mess. They just point it out.

The pointing draws attention, and the attention can turn to denial and self-protection and defensiveness if I want it to. This is where most of us stop. This is where we meet a friend for coffee and they nod their head and affirm our sin—*you are justified*, our friends say.

Or—it can transform into something else.

What if my sin weighed more than my pain?

The more I confess my frail humanity, the louder I hear the sound of another voice rising up in me, one that has some weight behind it. It is the voice of Hope, and Hope speaks with courage and a bit of a laugh. Because when those things we most fear will happen actually happen, we have a unique window of opportunity to take inventory of the battlefield in the aftermath. We look around, blink our eyes, listen to the quiet, and think to ourselves, *I am not dead. That did not kill me after all.*

How could it? If I say I'm a believer (and I am) and if I believe the Bible is true (and I do), then I have already died to that old life, the one that gropes and clings to the assurance and acceptance the world has to offer.

Christ stretched out arms on the cross, wide open to the words and attacks of the critic, wide open to my sin-desire to be my own little god, wide open to receive the insults and the insulted, the sin of the offense and the sin of my defensiveness.

He was stretched out so I could be free.

Crooked is no longer my shape.

And so if I have died with Christ and been raised to life in him, how can I die again at the hands of the critic? What have I to fear if death is no longer a risk?

The critic carries gifts he never meant to bring, motivation he has no awareness of. The voice of the critic forces us to face our biggest fears and, in so doing, listen for the voice of God. If we dare to believe Christ's dying and rising back up apply even in this, we can then be oddly, ironically, deliriously free.

> And since we died with Christ, we know we will also live with
> him. We are sure of this because Christ was raised from the

dead, and he will never die again. Death no longer has any power over him. (Rom. 6:8–9)

The critic points out my weaknesses, but he also forces me to draw a circle around what I believe.

- I believe in the power of life.
- I believe in the holy resurrection.
- I believe nothing can separate me from the love of God.
- I believe I have been given a spirit of power, love, and a sound mind.
- I believe the Son has set me free and I am free indeed.

When the email shows up at the end of the day, I can tell from the subject line that it will be combative. I have the worst kind of sinking feeling in my stomach—but it isn't what you think. My stomach sinks and flips in dread, not only because I'm worried what this person will say or think of me.

It's quite worse.

I'm dreading how this person's words will remind me of the crooked shape of my flesh. I'm dreading how I know I'm going to have to come face-to-face with the ugliness of my own sin, my own desire to be my own god, my fist clenching around the edges of my reputation and my good intentions and all of my excuses.

It doesn't mean I'll agree with this critic, or even that I'll respond.

It *does* mean I will be forced to move through all the stages of defensiveness, all the reasons why I don't deserve their critique, all the reasons why they're wrong. But soon, if I'm brave enough to admit what it is I really fear, I will eventually be brought down to my knees no matter what they say.

Here is where the mystery meets the mundane. Here is the place where the ordinary peers through the glass dimly, where even though I stand alone in my kitchen or sit waiting on the phone or stretch out on top of the covers, I can be there at the cross. That even though I am offended, I do not have to take offense. Instead of standing up tall and tensing my shoulders, I can bow down low and remember I have died.

And in that quiet, lowly place so close to the ground, I can finally see the grass, small blades, green and strong, born from the death of a seed. And life shoots up from broken earth carrying truth, joy, freedom. Because if I have died, then what have I to fear? And so from death, I live.

There is color coming up from the brown dirt.

There is hope in the despair.

There is art even in the midst of the last place I would choose to be.

See the Real Reason for Your Mediocre Art

Most of the time, the art others make—their homes, their food, their books, their beautifully inspired work—walks next to me like a comfortable friend. The million little ways God comes out of them inspires the life of God in me. I am open to their influence, small in their presence, and happy to be so. When I am free and in good places, I trust their art and look to them to learn more of myself.

Even though watching fellow image bearers come alive in their element on earth can be inspiring, there are those other times when their homes, their food, their books, and all that beautifully inspired work stands heavy on my chest. And just when I find a way to breathe shallow under the weight of it, when I squeeze out an extra hour of work, when I think I've got a crazy wide-eyed plan to catch up, *they start to jump on my rib cage with all their successes.*

Sometimes my biggest enemy isn't the critic spitting rude in my face, it's the artist crafting beautiful, gracious work by my side.

I read the inspiring words other people write and I get a hole in my stomach. That hole is a drain where inspiration and courage swirl around like dirty water, faster and faster until they disappear forever, leaving me alone and dejected in a land where I am a loser with nothing to say.

When you have a message and you pack words around that message like clay on a wheel and someone else shows up with a finished pot? It can feel like dying a little bit. Every artist knows this. It's why people stop making art.

Instead of being a friend, their art becomes the enemy and I'm certain their good work guarantees I will never work again. The more I think of how much they are shipping and launching and producing and unveiling, the less I'm able to breathe.

I'm no longer an image bearer with a job to do. I have become a job doer with an image to maintain.

Can we just call this what it is? Sin. Even the vocational artists who speak nothing of bearing the image of God know how toxic this thinking is.

Nobody's music is the enemy of your music. . . . The idea that someone else has made it when they shouldn't have made it is toxic thinking.[2]

John Mayer, to students at the Berkley College of Music

When the art others make begins to terrify rather than motivate, it means you are normal. But if you want to create art that matters, something has to change. And the number one thing that works for me is to stop.

The art has become too important. It is time to sink again.

It seems counterintuitive to stop just when you've convinced yourself you are already so very far behind. But stopping is really the only answer, because to carry on is to become a manic workaholic. To carry on is to worship the art rather than the Artist with a capital *A*. To carry on is to be pushed around by fear.

While taking a class he taught, I had the opportunity to sit down with Larry Crabb and his wife, Rachael. I shared with them my frantic worry about my deadline for this book you're reading now. As I did, they listened thoughtfully and then Larry said his vision for me is rest. *Rest? Are you kidding me? I just told you all the work I have to do!*

But something deep down in the center of my spirit knew he was right. That's why when the word "rest" left his lips, tears immediately showed up in my eyes.

When tears show up, we would do well to pay attention.

How can I rest in the midst of all there is to do?

That is precisely why you must.

Fear drives out the love. When you work from fear, there is no love in your work. And we don't want your loveless art.

So give the world and yourself a gift, and stop.

You are the beloved. So take some time to be the loved.

The fact that you need time to be the loved means you are human. And we want art that comes from human hands inspired by a capable God. Otherwise you will make medio-cre art at best.

If mediocre art is your goal, here are fourteen ways to achieve it:

- Make love to fear
- Apologize a lot
- Try to measure your impact
- Wait to feel qualified
- Compare yourself
- Fear the success of others
- Stay comfortable
- Have imaginary conversations with your critics
- Hold on to regret
- Keep impossible standards for perfection
- Demand appreciation
- Be easily offended
- Think there is only one right way to do it
- And by all means, don't take a risk

I don't want to make mediocre art and I don't want to live a mediocre life. I recently took a walk through my neighbor-hood and I noticed the connection between the way I walk and the way I live. I tend to walk distracted, listen to music, think through the tasks waiting for me when I get back home. I'm learning how to walk like a believer, how to look ahead on the path rather than just at my feet. How to stop and touch the bark on that funny-looking tree. How to see.

I found a leaf as big as my face, plucked it off the branch, and brought it home to show the kids. They were delighted because I was. We teach them how to see too.

Can we change our mind about our real goal? Getting in touch with the art that is alive within you isn't about you making something new. Instead, you have the uniquely human opportunity to re-imagine what already is.

Our imaginations are endless. You get to frame things in a way only you can, with a voice only you have. Sure, we may be framing the same thing, but we'll do it differently.

See the world as one of abundance rather than scarcity. I pulled that leaf off the tree and I didn't feel a bit wrong in doing it. The tree was full of them. There is enough to go around. There really is. Just because he is saying something you want to say doesn't mean you shouldn't say it too. If they do it, join them. If she says it, support her. If they are saying it too, all that means is that you're on to something. *This is a good thing*. Use it.

The world needs you awake and alive. Does the world need another book? Song? Painted living room? Not necessarily. But the world does need you to come alive right where you are and not where you wish you were. If writing books or songs or painting living rooms is what makes you come alive, then that's what you'll need to do.

See Your Wounds from Higher Up

We've grown up with the critics, though we haven't always called them that. Sometimes we call them Mom. Grandma. Mean kid in the cafeteria. Cool girls at the football game. That guy who took your job. That woman who took your husband. That person who lives in your head and shares your name.

The job that was supposed to be yours, *wasn't*. The man who was supposed to stay, *left*. The house that was supposed to sell, *won't*. What do we do when the stories that were supposed to be aren't? Sometimes the life that was supposed to be full feels empty. The answers that were supposed to be easy come difficult.

There may be legitimate cause to bend, to break down, to remain hard, hurt, a victim. There may be a thousand reasons to stay in your pain, unwilling or unable to let go. You can stop there, if you want to. But whole only comes after broken. Healing only comes after wounds. Are you willing to go a bit further and see?

> By his wounds we are healed. But they are our wounds, too; and until we have been healed we do not know what wholeness is. The discipline of creation, be it to paint, compose, write, is an effort toward wholeness. . . . How many artists, in the eyes of the world, have been less than whole? The great artists have gained their wholeness through their wounds, their epilepsies, tuberculosis, periods of madness.[3]
>
> Madeleine L'Engle, *Walking on Water*

The Great Artist—the Maker of stars and straw and soil— was not supposed to be a carpenter. He was supposed to be a king. To reign strong, not sweat blood. To be served, not be a servant. To live long, not die a criminal. If we stopped there, with his death, the story would be unjust and unfair—and unfinished. And that is precisely the point.

Perhaps living into the fullness of who you really are is partially about learning to see beyond what is to what could be. Could it be there is more to the story that we don't know

104

yet? It doesn't mean that God is trying to teach us a lesson in our difficulty. Perhaps he is simply creating a masterpiece.

God made the world, we messed it up, and then he came down to make it right again. He isn't a principal, he's an artist. He doesn't condemn, he creates. *But sometimes we stop too soon.* And when we do, things seem unjust. Perhaps they are simply *unfinished.* When the world tries to change you with its painful, cutting ways, instead embrace the story, receive grace, turn around, and change the world by deciding to see things differently.

How we respond when confronted with the critics has the potential to be the most beautiful art we'll ever make—we have the capacity to reflect the relational glory of God no matter who we're with, what we're doing, or what's gone wrong. This is when art is a verb rather than a noun. It isn't something you point to, it's a way you live.

7

listen

Look Beneath

If God is speaking, then nothing else matters but listening.

—Brennan Manning

The cicadas let their scratchy bellows loose, a chorus of a thousand squeaky doors always moving, never closing, never oiled, never stopping for a breath. Their strange song lingers familiar in my mind, a prelude to summer.

When I studied to become a sign language interpreter, one of the activities we did in class was to practice listening. The instructor set a timer for two minutes, and we wrote down everything we heard.

The ticking clock.

The movement of lead on paper.

Distant laughter from the classroom down the hall.

A flushing toilet.

A sneeze.

My paper filled up fast and I saw a list of all the things a Deaf student would miss if they sat in here with us.

They miss all these things because they can't hear.

What are the things I'm missing because I don't know how to listen?

Am I missing hints of my unique design? Am I lacking connection with fellow believers because I'm afraid of my pain and my questions? As you sink into the grace and knowledge of God and see the gifts brought by the critic, perhaps you will be open to listening differently.

Paying Attention

By the time I met Melissa during my junior year of college, her mom had already died. She was a year younger than me but seemed a little older since she was already married. Her mom made it to their wedding, but she didn't have much time left after that.

Later she told me she didn't cry much when her mom died. She couldn't find the emotion to go along with the heartbreak of losing her. She couldn't reach it, grab hold of it, and move it up to the surface. It was too deep. And so it came as a great surprise to her when she discovered herself in a heap of blubbering, slobbery emotion during the movie *You've Got Mail.*

It was easier for her to cry for Kathleen Kelly and the last days of her mother's dream, The Shop Around the Corner, than it was for her to access those tears for her own real-life mother. Madeleine L'Engle puts into words for us a very simple truth of why that is:

> In art, either as creators or participators, we are helped to remember some of the glorious things we have forgotten, and some of the terrible things we are asked to endure, we who are children of God by adoption and grace.[1]

Art makes it possible for us to remember both the beauty and the horrific, the lovely and the loss. Art numbs the wound just enough for us to be able to access the source of it, to reach down into the depths and pull it up to examine.

The beauty of art is that it separates us enough from our own pain in order to make it safe to approach. This movie, this novel, this musical, this song isn't my story, and so I can freely let myself identify with it. In the freedom, the tears have permission to fall. And in the tear-fall, I realize that this movie, this novel, this musical, this song holds pieces of my story after all.

Maybe it's the same way for other kinds of art we make.

As important as it is to embrace the gifts you have and the unique ways you can offer hope to others, you also need to recognize and embrace what brings out the hope in you.

What touches your soul so deeply that it causes tears to come out? We're talking about *magic water that pours out of our eyes.* Maybe paying attention to what calls that water forth will give us a hint as to what it is that makes us come alive.

Listen to Your Tears

There is a painting—finished, unique, complete houses lifted up by strings out of chaotic rubble—and when I saw it, my eyes filled up unexpectedly. The concept is too good, the visual stays with me—redemption and hope captured on canvas. I wipe a rogue tear and wonder where it comes from.

This morning, I read a blog post by Amber Haines. She wrote about being overcome with her life gifts. It is lovely, as her posts always are. And then I read how her husband baptized their young son and called him brother as he lowered him into the water, "I baptize you, Isaac, my son and my brother." A father, loving his son. It's that word, *brother*. That's what brings the tears. This time they don't stop.

In line to board an airplane, I hear a man behind me say, "Now remember, it's just up and down from here." I can't help but turn to look, the scruff in his voice not matching the gentle words he speaks.

She smiles and nods okay several times, and I know she has some type of disability, though I can't place it. He isn't boarding the plane, must have special permission to escort her to the gate. She looks excited, like this is all very new for her, like perhaps she's never done anything alone, ever. The man (her brother?) looks hesitant to let her go. But he assures her *it's just up and down from here*, as if perhaps they've had conversations about this trip for a long time before now.

He is concerned for her. I am surprised by the sting in my eyes.

I read these lines in *When Crickets Cry* by Charles Martin: "Final words are hard to hear when you know for certain they are indeed final. And I knew for certain. Four anniversaries had come and gone while I remained in this nowhere place. Even the crickets were quiet."[2] Even though it's fiction, it isn't really. I think of my mother-in-law, her husband sick with cancer. Magic water.

I sit in front of cameras for live television with Moira Brown in Canada and things are going well and honest, and then she reads the dedication of my first book out loud, *For John, who lives and breathes the mystery of Christ in you, the hope of glory*. I think I hide it well, and I don't think you can tell, but hearing his name and knowing the mystery brings hot, quick tears to the surface, right there on live TV.

When you listen to a friend tell her story, it isn't enough to say you cried while listening. When you watch a movie that brings out emotion in you, consider the moment the tears rushed up with stinging fingers, circling around your eyes. Pay attention to the word or phrase that called the magic water out. What is the word you would use to describe how you feel in that moment? What is the memory it brings to mind? How deep does this well really go?

Why does it matter what makes you cry or tear up? Maybe it just means you're overly emotional, sappy, too sensitive. Maybe.

Or maybe our tears are tiny messengers, secret keepers of the most vulnerable kind, sent to deliver a most important message—*Here is where your heart beats strong. Here is a hint to your design. Here is a gift from your inner life, sent to remind you of those things that make you come alive.*

These tears carry the gift of your desire. Listen to them.

Change in the world comes when we acknowledge what moves us and why. It could be injustice or a sunset by the river or the Super Bowl. I don't know what it is for you, but you need to know. What else in all of creation can shed tears?

Listen to what makes you cry.

Listen to Your Questions

When I am worried about things beyond my control, I desperately need to go outside—to drink my coffee on the back deck, to sit on the bench in the front yard, to lean back on the warm concrete at dusk, to chat with a neighbor on our painted porch steps, to take a walk.

If your life is filled with questions and you go on a walk demanding answers, you may come home with two hands filled with disappointment. But oh, the peace to be found in learning to carry around your questions, in learning, as Ruth Haley Barton says, to "be with what is." Let the day be the day without trying to run away from it.

Questions used to scare me. As teachers explained assignments in school, if I had a question I would hold out to the bitter end, ever so hopeful someone else would ask it.

The summer after my sophomore year of college, I remember reading a verse about grace, though I don't remember exactly which one. I do know the verse confused me, made me question if I really understood what grace was at all. I had a lot of questions about it, and those questions became a lifelong journey into uncovering the deeper truths of the gospel in my personal life.

But those questions also led me to write my first book. The book was part of my art, but the deeper work was the change that happened within my soul, the way the grace of God woke something up within me that was there but hadn't yet been uncovered. And all of that started with a question about something I didn't understand.

Pay attention to your questions. They may carry more answers within them than you are able to see at first glance—though perhaps not the kind of answers you're looking for. I obviously can't say I have all the answers to my questions about grace. But I can say I have become more fully myself as I've asked them.

Listen to Your Heartbreak

Just like the things that bring us to tears carry with them hints to our design, so do the things that break our hearts. Listening to the pain of loss and heartbreak can wake us up to who we are, where we come from, and what matters most. But only if we open ourselves up to them.

I am more comfortable closing myself off from the things that break my heart. When I see the hungry children on TV, I turn the channel. But we can't turn ourselves away from our life moments. We must turn toward them and walk into them no matter how badly we wish we could turn the channel.

In the summer of 2010, John's dad, Frank, was diagnosed with lung cancer. There was hope he could beat it and he did all of the necessary treatments to try. I remember looking into

John's tired eyes shortly after Frank's diagnosis, whispering knowing words—*This is going to be a tough year*. We knew we were beginning to learn what it meant to live with heartbreak, struggle, and certain death.

Time molds and kneads life into different shapes as we go along. We feel brave and then we get scared. We feel honest and then we hide. Things are going well and then the doctor calls.

February of 2011 was when I received the invitation from Compassion International to travel with a group of bloggers to the Philippines. I was to join their team as a writer with the purpose of raising awareness about the needs of children living in poverty around the world.

It took me two weeks to say yes. There was already so much heaviness at home, I couldn't bear the thought of flying across the world only to gather more of it.

A few days before we were scheduled to leave, John whispered in the dark as he pulled back the sheets, *You'll come back changed*. He spoke it in love, meant to be encouraging, but all I could do was cry. I didn't want the pain of change. I wanted to stay home and make spaghetti.

Our trip was in May and I traveled all day from North Carolina to California where I met my team for the first time. Twenty minutes after we shook hands and made small talk, it was time to board the biggest plane I had ever seen in real life. It had stairs, is all I'm saying. As I sat on the tarmac at LAX more than a little nervous over the upcoming twelve-hour flight, I called John from my cell phone, my last chance to talk to him before our plane headed to Japan and then Manila.

His voice sounded distant and detached. "Dad isn't doing well"—he was rushed, overwhelmed—"Stella is struggling at school. Her stomachaches aren't going away. She misses you."

I wanted to die. I held the phone as close to my face as I could, watched as the baggage handlers tossed bags into the heavy belly of the plane, felt fear hurl itself into my own belly with as much force and carelessness. I leaned my forehead against the plastic-y glass of the airplane window and cradled my phone, my only connection to normal.

There I was, willingly sitting on a gigantic skyscraper with wings, nose pointed toward the Pacific Ocean, preparing to shoot through the sky to Asia in this time-traveling capsule, and my family was all the way on the East Coast of the US, sick and needing me, one of them literally dying. Looking back on it now, the panic attack that ensued five hours into our flight should have come as no surprise.

I didn't feel capable of handling the poverty I was about to witness in the Philippines. But are any of us ever capable of handling the pain of this broken life? Isn't that why Christ had to come?

Seeing the neediness and brokenness and poverty of the world and of my own soul could shut me down if I let it. But Christ has made it possible for me to open up.

Henri Nouwen speaks to this in his book *Here and Now*:

> The more I think about the human suffering in our world and my desire to offer a healing response, the more I realize how crucial it is not to allow myself to become paralyzed by feelings of impotence and guilt. More important than ever is to be very faithful to my vocation to do well the few things I am called to do and hold on to the joy and peace

they bring me. I must resist the temptation to let the forces of darkness pull me into despair and make me one more of their many victims.[3]

What Nouwen says here is crucial if we want to see the relevance of living our lives as artists—he says in the face of human suffering and heartbreak it is *more important than ever* to be faithful to our vocation and our art. In the presence of heartbreak, it is more important than ever to be who we uniquely are, bearing the image of God in the world.

I experienced this in a profound way while in the Philippines. We spent our days walking through the dirty, dire streets of Manila, holding hands with children who lived in houses that cannot even bear the name by any real definition. They lived in square spaces with garbage walls, surrounded by darkness, wet pavement, dirty animals, waste. We spent our days visiting their homes and seeing the work Compassion is doing on their behalf. And then we spent our evenings writing.

We wrote what we saw, we shared photos and stories and then, we hit publish. And in that moment, our collective words, stories, and images were available for anyone to read and see what we were seeing. We invited readers to sponsor children and the miracle is, they did. I could not move to the Philippines and adopt every child I saw. I could not offer the medical treatment they needed. I could not clean up their streets where they lived or the hearts of their abusers. But I could write.

It wasn't a lot and it wasn't enough, but it was one of the million little ways I believe God wanted to bring light into a dark place. *Come, see what I've been doing,* I sensed him say as I walked through those streets. *Come, see where I live.* So I went, and I saw, and then, he said, *Now tell them.*

So I wrote about it.[4]

I didn't feel qualified and my writing wasn't perfect. But that week in the Philippines, I learned a little more what it means to sink into God and to trust him to do what he does—first within me and then through me, for his glory and the benefit of others.

It doesn't always work out that way, though. My natural inclination during those times when my heart is breaking isn't to make art and to offer myself to the world as I am. My natural inclination is to make a chocolate cake, to eat that cake in front of the TV, to hide myself under a furry blanket, and to cruise mindlessly through my Instagram feed. My natural inclination is to escape, shut down, shut out, and close up.

Frank died one month after I returned from the Philippines. In the end, it was eleven months from diagnosis to the day of his funeral. The family rode in the backseat of a black Cadillac to the grave where he would be buried. No one wanted to be there. Who would? We sat small under that tent in our Sunday best, watching dust return to dust in the middle of hot July.

But life keeps right on, and we celebrate because there is much to celebrate. We swallow down joy in big, breathless gulps. And then, we grieve when it all gets to be too much, and that is as it should be.

I have a deep appreciation for the work and research of Brené Brown. In her book *The Gifts of Imperfection*, she points out the importance of embracing heartbreak as well as joy:

There's no such thing as selective emotional numbing. There is a full spectrum of human emotions and when we numb the dark, we numb the light. While I was "taking the edge off" of the pain and vulnerability, I was also unintentionally dulling my experiences of good feelings, like joy.[5]

I don't believe we have to have pain to make beautiful art—but when the pain comes, an artist knows she must face it. Grief does deep, important, sacred work. We have to pay attention to what grieves us and be willing to be fully human, both in what makes us come alive and in what has the capacity to shut us down. What breaks our hearts reminds us what is deeply important to us. It is often from this place that our most beautiful, honest, generous art comes. As we move into the world as who we most deeply, fully are, our art has the capacity to be a gift for others, and in this we see hints of the resurrection life.

Listen to Your Tuesdays

Tuesday is the most sensible day of the week. Monday has the heavy job of shouldering the blame for the world's bad mood. Sunday is all slow-cooked rest, Wednesday cheers us on with a halfway banner, and Thursday, aside from being the best night for TV, is basically a bright green arrow to the weekend. Is it even necessary to bring up the weekend days? How they play carefree, plan parties, host celebrations, and fancy nights out? Weekend days are lazy and spontaneous and gather up with friends and family.

But for all the ways I try to picture him differently, Tuesday is a perfectly ordinary, no-fuss, introverted day.

No one says, "Thank God it's Tuesday!"

But there is something ordinary about Tuesday that attracts me.

Maybe it's a different day for you, but consider what this ordinary day represents. Here is where you keep time, in this home with these people and this skin on. Here is the leftover chicken soup in the fridge, the grout in the bathroom that won't come clean, your favorite corner of the sofa. Here, on this ordinary Tuesday, is where we learn to be human.

This is how we live. This is what we eat. This is where we planted the tulip bulbs with a soup spoon in November and watched them bloom in spring. This table holds the memories of a thousand dinner stories, these chairs wear the stains of their jelly and Play-Doh hands. This house was made a home the first night we slept here, the night I cried because the windows had no coverings and neither did my heart.

> Our lives are at once ordinary and mythical. We live and die, age beautifully or full of wrinkles. We wake in the morning, buy yellow cheese, and hope we have enough money to pay for it. At the same instant we have these magnificent hearts that pump through all sorrow and all winters we are alive on the earth. We are important and our lives are important, magnificent really, and their details are worthy to be recorded.[6]
>
> Natalie Goldberg, *Writing Down the Bones*

When we resist living within our ordinary days, we are in danger of losing a sense of ourselves. We don't need to walk away from our routines and daily rhythms to find something more interesting. More often we need to wake up *to* them. Hold the minutes of Tuesday morning in your hand, turn them over with the local paper, carry them into the office, the cafeteria, the studio.

This is where you live and where your people live.

This is the house of God.

Thank God it's Tuesday.

Listen to Your Crazy Ideas

The Grammys were on recently and it was a rare night of having the house to myself. I watched the red carpet preshow because I could and the dresses were pretty. An interviewer asked one of the bands what their secret was as they walked into the theater. Their answer? "We just keep chasing our craziest ideas."

Crazy ideas don't always mean a ticket to the Grammys. But maybe tickets to the Grammys only come to those who first chased a crazy idea. Same goes for the Oscar winner, the moon walker, the airplane flier, the actor president, the single mom with a little book about a boy wizard named Harry. And then there was the pregnant virgin, the shepherd king, the baby Savior, the clear water turning merlot red while the guests laughed and danced into the night.

As we begin to embrace our own sense of place and time in our Tuesdays, maybe we will be more open to considering our crazy ideas. With your feet planted firmly in the soil of home, allow yourself the freedom to dream a little.

I think perhaps everyone has crazy ideas but most people are afraid to consider them. There are a rare few who pursue them, but they wouldn't realize it, because to them, they aren't crazy ideas. They're just *ideas.*

But for those of us who have a dream tucked away in our back pocket, perhaps it's time to bend our ear toward the craziest of our ideas and hear what they have to say.

Over the years, that dream may have taken on many different names in your mind: *Silly. Ridiculous. Hobby. Foolish. Impossible. Waste of time.* You have called it names for so long that perhaps you have never actually taken the time to consider how it got there in your pocket in the first place.

We throw trash away; we don't put trash in our pockets. Your dream is there because at one time you saw its value. And so you tucked it away for safekeeping. But doubt and fear have convinced you to keep it hidden, convinced you to rename that dream *Wrong.*

What would it take for you to pull your dream out again, to stop taunting it with cruel names, and to simply listen to what it has to say? No filters. No back talk. No eye rolls. Dare to handle it, to hold it in your hands and consider it with kindness and compassion.

You may not be sure what will come of the dream. But might you be willing to develop a small but respectable amount of reverence for the way God speaks to you through your desires?

What is your moon, your airplane, your boy-wizard book? What is your brave lyric, your odd first chapter, your new business motto? What is your crazy idea? No, not your perfect idea. Not your logical, well-planned, power-pointed practical idea. There's a place for those too. But many times the most logical ideas *start out crazy.* What is your crazy idea and what should you do with it?

Maybe you should chase it.

Now—what if your crazy idea is to leave your wife and pursue some grand adventure of your choosing? What if your crazy idea is to embezzle money from your employer or abandon your kids for the sake of your career? What if, when you realize your deepest desire, you also realize it is to do something wrong? Should you chase it?

Well, of course not. But why? You might be tempted to say, *well, because that violates the law of God. It's sin.* Chasing a desire that will lead to doing something wrong *is* sin. But be very careful with your wording. The point isn't that you would then be violating the law of God—we already know we can't keep his law. The point now, as a new covenant believer, is that you would be violating the *love* of God, and that is a different motivation altogether.

If you are a person who has received the sacrifice of Jesus in your place and who has a spirit united with his Spirit, then your greatest purpose is to reveal his glory and your greatest grief is to violate his love.

Remember why you came to him in the first place. Remember why you were moved toward him when you realized his heart was moved toward you. If you don't fully believe true life is found in the one way of Jesus, then listening to your desire will ultimately lead you away from him, not toward him. But if you are a believer with a new heart, remember the gift of love and move into the world as the person you fully are.

There were only ten seconds left on our listening assignment. My classmates and I took the assignment seriously, so the room was quiet as we worked. My hand began to cramp as I tried to finish writing down all the sounds I heard. When we began, I thought for certain I wouldn't hear enough to fill up half a page, much less write without stopping for two minutes. When our professor hit her stopwatch, I looked over the filled-up page with all of the noises and commotion I heard in a two-minute span of time.

Only when we decided to quiet ourselves and listen on purpose did we really begin to hear.

The first half of this book has been like that listening exercise I did in college, a practice of quieting the soul in the midst of distraction and obligation to hear what we may otherwise have missed.

Now that we've spent some time uncovering where we've been, who we are, who God is, and what we're up against, it's time to consider what it means to move into the world as an artist.

I'm sure this uncovering is not complete, but I hope it is at least partial. Do you know you are an image bearer with a job to do? As you continue to consider the art you were born to make, what will it look like for you to release the art you were made to live?

release the art
you were made to live

The beauty of God demands a response from us.
—Michael Card, *Scribbling in the Sand*

Anytime we begin to uncover hints of our design, the challenge is to know whether or not we can trust it. We confronted these questions before, but now that we are more fully awake to our unique design, the questions come around again: *How do I know this isn't just me? Am I making this stuff up? Is it selfish to pursue desire?*

When we finally admit there is something within us worth offering, when we finally recognize we have the ability, privilege, and calling to influence our families, our workmates, our neighbors, and our world in a way only we can, there may still be one statement that comes heavy with question: *I don't feel qualified for the job.*

Consider the men left behind after Jesus' resurrection, entrusted with the task of sharing The Most Important Truth Ever with a broken world.

> When they saw the courage of Peter and John and realized that they were unschooled, ordinary men, they were astonished and they took note that these men had been with Jesus. (Acts 4:13 NIV)

Aren't we all Peter and John, unschooled and ordinary when it comes to the things that matter—things of influence, relationship, and heart? When these men in Acts 4 spoke with boldness and clarity, the leaders were stunned. But the source of their astonishment did not rest on the shoulders of these two men. The people who heard Peter and John traced their courage back to a greater source—*these men have been with Jesus.* These two image bearers spoke from a place deep within themselves, a place of courage and conviction. They carried God's image into the world as the men they uniquely were— for the glory of God and the benefit of others.

> Have you ever felt like your dream was too big for you?
> Moses felt that way more than once. When God called him to lead the Israelites out of the land of Egypt, Moses felt like it was too big. He felt like he wasn't qualified, so he asked God to send someone else to do it. In my experience,

you'll never feel qualified. But God doesn't call the qualified;
God qualifies the called.[1]

Mark Batterson, *The Circle Maker*

When it comes to releasing the art we were made to live,
we have to remember we carry within us the same Spirit
as did Moses and Peter and John. Their words left an im-
pression, something worth remembering. They carried the
aroma of Christ with them wherever they went, and they did
it because there was something alive within them—rather
Someone.

Are we willing to join the souls of the ordinary?

Can we possibly live from our wholeness rather than our
dysfunction? Can we decide now to stop waiting for qualifi-
cation, permission, and approval? Can we begin to trust that
the God who lives within us weaves his Spirit around ours
so intensely, so completely, and with such intimacy that our
desires are actually beginning to look like his?

In part 2, we considered five places to look to uncover the
art that is alive within us. We did not set off on a journey to
find our art; rather, we stood in the place where we already
are and began to uncover it. A tree has roots that burrow
deep into the soil, but it also has leaves and branches that are
seen and exposed to the wind. The leaves of the tree reveal
something of its roots.

Moving into part 3, consider what it is you have uncovered
and what it might mean for you to release it into your world.
What is alive within you that you can now give to someone
else? What does it look like for the artist to move into her
world fully alive and available?

We have identified the roots. Now it's time to find out what kind of blooms this tree wants to bear. The practices in the remaining chapters are not meant to be followed like a list or even in any particular order.

Reject the temptation to believe you need to wait for a new set of life circumstances, a different job, or a new setting. Being who you already are no matter the circumstance of your life is what it means to release the art you were made to live. Respond to God where you are *as you are.* Now I want to offer you five practices that might help you do that.

8

show up

Creativity is not about me. It is not about you. It is not us somehow acting like little gods, creating on our own in the same way God creates. . . . The most we can hope for is to respond appropriately and creatively to who God is and what he means. Creativity is a response.

—Michael Card, *Scribbling in the Sand*

She comes right on time, if there even is such a thing when it comes to babies. They come when they're ready if we're lucky. Or if you're me, they come early and face the wrong way.

But this tiny girl comes the week they planned for, right in the middle of summer. You can't always predict North

Carolina weather, but one thing you can know for sure is summer will be hot. I make my way across the steaming asphalt in the lot near the visitor's entrance. My camera bag is heavy on my shoulder, but I'm thankful to have it. It's important to me to get better-than-phone photos when I get my first glimpse of my new niece.

John and the kids arrived ahead of me, so the whole family is gathered in the waiting room. They crowd around the window in the corner and the entire room seems to move with the rhythm of new life. I ease my way through the tightly gathered group, manage to find a spot behind the smallest ones to aim my camera through the glass. I catch a glimpse of my brother-in-law on the other side, bent low over his tiny girl, eyes full with gratitude as he takes her in.

There she is, all red soft wonder, brand new but mysteriously familiar. Like we know her. Like she belongs with us.

There are her mama's full lips, just as we expected. There is her grandmother's round face, those hands like her sister's. She is inspected from dark hair to pink heel, compared and measured against every relative we know of. And when we find a feature we don't recognize, we agree without much discussion that those must have come from some distant relative none of us remember.

Looking back, I wonder why we did that. New life comes into the world and we insist every part of her must resemble someone else. But what about that shock of long lash like no one we know, those toes we haven't quite seen before? These new features belong only to her, and she has arrived on her hot July stage debuting these gifts to the world for the very first time.

Here I am, a tiny wonder, bearing the image of God and of you. But I bring some of myself here as well, some that belongs only to me. See me as I am, receive what I have to offer.

She may reflect familiar, but she shows up as a poem, *the poiema of God*, completely new, woven inside her mother, imagined in the mind of Christ.

So did I.

So did you.

We arrived here as art and we spend our lives uncovering the beauty we have to offer—not just the work of our hands but the shape of our hearts. We are here as expressions of God to reflect his glory in the world. As the community of humanity, we will do that in a million different little ways. There is no formula to living life with Christ. There is only showing up as we are, trusting he is not only with us but within us, and believing he wants to come out.

Show Up as a Poet

In his book *Orthodoxy*, G. K. Chesterton makes a pretty good argument that the poets of the world understand the beauty of life more freely than do those who are always trying to figure things out.

> Poetry is sane because it floats easily in an infinite sea; reason seeks to cross the infinite sea, and so make it finite. The result is mental exhaustion . . . To accept everything is an exercise, to understand everything a strain. The poet only desires exaltation and expansion, a world to stretch himself in. The poet only asks to get his head into the heavens. It is

the logician who seeks to get the heavens into his head. And it is his head that splits.[1]

It is enough to think about for a long time. I can't say I fully understand all the implications of what he says here, but it stirs something in me that I can't easily let go. I consider what living life like a poet might mean.

The girls asked me to come read to their class today.

I pull into the school parking lot, *Ivy and Bean* tucked into my purse, anxiety pulsing in my chest. I sign in at the computer in the office, think about living art and what it means for a mom frazzled in the lobby. I walk slowly through the hallway, savor the quiet before the third grade eyes find me.

What does it mean to live life like an artist in the midst of this everyday hustle?

The question brings a shift. The word *poet* comes to mind.

I realize I am clenching my jaw, moving to the next thing like a chess player. I'll make this move and then this will happen. I am in control of everything.

In this small moment standing outside their classroom, I am compelled to approach these next few moments like they are lines in a poem rather than items on my agenda.

I don't feel overwhelmed with the responsibility to do this in everything.

Just in this one thing, right now.

I don't know exactly what it means, but the mystery of the concept draws me in. I stand in this one moment and for the next twenty of them, I have agreed to read to the class. This, right here, is all my life is right now.

Emily, don't just show up with your body. Show up in your soul. Be fully alive. Let me be fully alive in you.

I do not change the world today. But I decide to show up where I already am. The God of the Universe lives in me on a Friday in their third grade classroom. There is much left undone at home, in the sink, on my laptop, in my heart. I don't feel ready to live like a poet.

In this, there is no ready. There is only belief.

Show up as a poet once, and chances are, you'll do it again.

Uncovering the art alive within me and releasing it into my world is what it means to worship God. Showing up in their classroom is worship when I do it as the person I fully am. Living as an artist profoundly affects how I relate in community with others.

This is what it looks like to take small steps toward the mystery. You aren't moving to figure things out or to catch up to an expectation, but you are moving because you are alive. You have a glimpse of what it might feel like to live life as an artist in the middle of your ordinary day.

You are aware of your desire for a map, but all you sense is a mystery. Instead of a plan, you are simply asked to show up in this day the same way you did the day you were born, with empty hands and an instinct to depend on someone bigger than you.

Show Up within Your Limits

We spent the morning taping videos, stopping and starting and stopping again. The work was slow but satisfying, the kind you prepare the best you can for but know you can only do so much beforehand.

We've finished lunch and it's time to get back to it. But before we do, I chat a bit with Duane, the videographer. "My favorite part," he says, "is getting home and looking at all the footage and seeing how it all goes together. There's always a point when I realize we missed a shot or didn't get everything I wanted to get. But that can be fun, because then I have to find ways to make what we have work."

He didn't get the right footage, enough shots, the best light. But that's when the *fun* starts?

My sister stands in front of her fireplace, whispers under her breath the things she dislikes about the angle, the mantel, the odd shape of the room, and placement of the windows. But she isn't discouraged by it. In fact, she seems *motivated* by it.

> Much of the beauty that arises in art comes from the struggle an artist wages with his limited medium.
>
> Henri Matisse

My son cries from the kitchen. I hear him crumble another paper, hit the table with a flat hand. "I messed up *again*!" There are at least four half-finished crayon-drawn airplanes strewn across the table. Not one of them fits the picture in his head.

A tall stack of white paper sits in front of him next to a clear jar filled with crayons in every color. Every time he "messes up" he knows there will be another sheet to draw on. He isn't forced to make any of them work.

I wonder what would happen if I gave him three crayons and one sheet of paper? I wonder if it would frustrate him more? Or if it would force him to be creative?

If we show up with hands filled with perfection, then why would we need to think at all? What would life ever require of us? There would be no need for creativity. A technician has missing pieces and can't continue the job. An artist knows that the mess-ups and the limits are where the fun begins.

> If we are to live our lives fully and well, we must learn to embrace the opposites, to live in a creative tension between our limits and our potentials. We must honor our limitations in ways that do not distort our nature, and we must trust and use our gifts in ways that fulfill the potentials God gave us.[2]
>
> Parker Palmer, *Let Your Life Speak*

Our limits can be gifts if we let them be. They might show up like failure, season of life, fatigue, disability, grief, burnout. But the limits tell us important things about ourselves. They help us draw lines for margin. They pave the way for vulnerability. They sometimes show us what our passion *isn't*. And that can be just as important as knowing what it *is*. In some cases, our limitations can actually become our inspiration.

Consider the way God creates. He is the Author of limitless potential, yet he chose men and women to live out his story in the world—God, who cannot be held back or contained, poured himself into skin and submitted himself to gravity and showed up, not just to live among us but to become one of us himself. He yielded himself to the humblest of positions in order to fulfill the greatest rescue mission in history.

Befriend narrow limits. Let them be a reminder to you that your work and your art are impossible without divine resources. You can do nothing on your own anyway. Be relieved to show up with all of your love as well as your insecurity, your skill as well as your fear. Show up in the world and be who you already are.

Show up human. Show up authentic. Show up right where you are, with two feet on your Tuesday. And when people say,

The sky's the limit! implying there is limitless potential and you can do anything you set your mind to, remember that's simply not true, and if it were true, I'm not sure it would be a good thing. When it comes to your influence and your ability to effect change, something has to be the limit other than the sky. Identify what those things are, set your own boundaries, and leave room for your soul to breathe.

Show Up, Ready or Not

Maybe you think it isn't the right time to show up. *I'm not ready to write that book, try for a baby, take that job, quit the one I've got.* There can be a real frustration for those who long to move but believe it isn't the right time.

Showing up where you are with what you have is all you can do. You have your two hands, your sick parents, the items on your to-do list. You have your extra deadlines, your diagnosis, the children at your table. You have been given your life, what you hold in your hands, the ground beneath your feet. You have been asked to show up. How do I know? Because you were born.

Maybe you have certain ideas about what it means to do your thing the right way. Maybe you're a writer or a musician or a painter, but you are stuck in a pattern of defeat.

Maybe you homeschool your babies or you teach in a public school classroom and your ideas of what it means to be a good teacher are keeping you from actually teaching.

Maybe you just got married and you have this idea about what a spouse is supposed to do and be and look like. But your unrealistic ideas are keeping you from seeing your lover.

And in the midst of all your try-hard effort to do love right, you are missing out on loving well.

Are you allowing your own expectations to hinder you from freely expressing yourself? Is your idea of *the right way* keeping you from *your best way*? Are you too distracted to show up? Are you living like a programmer instead of a poet?

Showing up doesn't necessarily imply readiness or preparation or an invitation, even. Showing up has simple implications: you are dressed, you are moving into the day, you have willing hands and an open heart. You are here.

It's true, it might not be the right time to do a certain thing, pursue a particular endeavor, or make a final decision. You may be in the middle of a long period of waiting, something we'll talk about in the next chapter. But a lot of times, we confuse readiness with courage.

We think that because we don't feel courageous, it means we aren't ready to show up. But courage is not the absence of fear. If you wait to feel courageous before you release your art, you might be waiting forever. When it comes to courage, we're often looking for the wrong emotion.

Courage is about more than simply believing in yourself, more than making art with confidence and living life without fear. Courage, I'm discovering, happens in the deep and secret place of the spirit, the place where my life is joined with God's. It feels more like a gift than an award, more like a strength that doesn't come from me. And the more we live from who we really are, the more courage will grow.

Courage starts small. Courage is crying before the conversation but moving toward it anyway. Courage is head bowed down low, hands open in surrender, heart broken and moved with compassion. Courage knows—*I can't do this on my own.* Courage turns to Christ, washes feet, steps out on top of the water. Courage comes back up after she sinks, brushes off knees after she falls.

We cannot wait until we feel courageous to make art or live art.

We make art and live art even as we wait for the courage to come.

Courage bleeds neediness.

Courage sees hope in dark places.

Courage leans heavy on Jesus and moves in the middle of fear.

Eight Statements Keeping You from Showing Up

People who are awake have a dangerous enemy. Jesus is the one way, but there are a million loud voices that keep us from the million little ways he wants to show up through us to the world. These voices speak against any beauty we long to believe exists within us.

Here are eight statements we say to ourselves that may be keeping us from living and releasing our art:

1. I'm not cut out for this. Two years ago when my first book came out, I had more radio interviews than I could keep track of. After one particularly bad one, this phrase came to mind: *I'm not cut out for this.*

I tried to distract myself with email and the laundry, but I couldn't ignore my shaking hands and the sweat under my armpits, turning my pink shirt darker pink. Finally I sat and tried to reason it away. *You've done countless interviews by now, why do you still get so nervous?*

Because I'm not cut out for this. And even as I said it, I heard what I can only describe as the Lord whisper, *No, you are not cut out. You have been placed in.* I really sensed those words, as sure as the way I stumbled and uh'd my way through that interview. He reminded me I have been placed into him. Not cut out at all.

It is one thing to know my limits—to recognize there are endeavors in the world that may be honorable and good but still aren't for me to pursue. But as we begin to embrace the art that is alive within us and release that art into the world around us, the critic in our head will speak loudly to threaten our unique design. Even in the things we know we are called to, there will be times when we feel as if we aren't cut out for them.

God takes great delight in finding us in places where we don't feel cut out to succeed. And that is where he sends his invitation of remembrance—my shaky, sweaty mess is a reminder that I am desperate to depend on a source other than myself.

2. Someone else can do it better. This happens in all kinds of art, the kind you live or make or speak into existence. Someone else can write better, love better, lead better, speak better, teach better, design better, parent better, or pray better. It's a courage stealer, a lie that attacks your image-bearing identity. There are two ways to combat it.

The first is to agree with it. *Yes, someone else can do it better, and they probably already have.* If you think you are the first one to say something true or do something well, you have bigger problems than being scared to show up. Agree that, yes, someone else can do it better.

The second way to combat this statement is to hear the wise words of my friend and counselor Steve Lynam, words he said to me when I shared with him how very defeated I felt in my lack of originality. "There is no new truth, dear. All truth belongs to God. Sometimes you simply need to hear someone else say it. That's what I hope I'm doing for you. And that's what your voice will be for them."

You may not be the first to say it, write it, create it, or believe it—but you saying it may be the first time someone finally hears. Yes, someone else can say it better, but that doesn't mean you can't say it too. Throw out your inhibitions and spin around in this crazy world of recycled ideas. There is nothing new to say. *Say it anyway.*

3. People might not like it. *See chapter 6.*

4. I have nothing to offer. This is a big one, where your art takes a huge hit. It isn't simply that you have something you want to offer but believe someone else can do it better. No, you actually believe you have nothing to offer *at all.*

Were you made on purpose? Is there a unique blend of interests, desire, wisdom, quirks, insecurities, and loves that are within you? Can we agree those things are not a coincidence?

Do you believe that the Holy Spirit of God, the same one who moved over the surface of the waters and moved out of heaven onto the surface of the land, has also moved into you, to take up residence in the innermost seat of your personality?

Could it also be that there are things in you that aren't in anyone else? That the way God has attached himself to you is a unique way he wants to display his glory to the world?

Do you believe in his power to bring life out of death? Could it also be possible, then, that he can bring life out of you? Could there be some corner of the room he wants to influence and you are the person he has called to do that? It may not look like what you expect it to look like or the way other people expect it to look.

You were made in the secret place, woven together on purpose with threads made from sacred longings that come not only from you but from the heart of God—he wove you together with a personality and you bring your own you-ness to the table.

I will admit it might take our whole lives to see the complete picture of what we can now see only in part. But don't believe for a minute that a person who bears the image of God has nothing to offer.

5. I hate my calling. Sometimes we refuse to show up, not because we doubt our calling, but because we *hate* our calling. I had a boxing match with the air in my shower this morning. I was frustrated because today I don't want writing to be my calling. I don't want to be vulnerable in a book. Why do I feel compelled to splay my weaknesses out on pages that live on bookstore shelves, bedside tables, car front seats, couch arms? Why can't I just write about food? Animals? The weather? Over the past two years, I have wished so many times that my passion was food.

A few weeks ago, I cried while reading a food blog. It wasn't because I was so hungry or because there was anything intrinsically tear-worthy in the avocado. Rather it was because the idea of writing about food was so comforting to me, so other-than what I write about, that reading it pulled up tears before I had a chance to figure out where they came from. *Oh, to write instead about tomato soup!*

I know every food writer reading these words is shaking their fist at me right now as I romanticize their work and assume they have less struggle than I do. Isn't that what we do when our calling infuriates us? We look at the calling of others and convince ourselves they have it easier.

And so I visit cooking blogs and make recipes and I feel safe and inspired. But those things don't make me come alive from the inside out. Talking about the grace of God and the art of his people makes me come alive. It's deep and it's serious and it's sometimes heavy. It's awkward to hold and it's too complicated for an elevator pitch. It's hard to market, difficult to summarize, cumbersome to share in the carpool line. But when I look into your eyes and I see you get it too, when we can talk about the things of Christ and the mystery of this hope of glory and how I believe he wants to show up uniquely in the lives of believers on earth—it's like someone turned on the music.

I would love to run from my work and get lost in a food blog. There is a time for that, to be quite sure. But I am grown-up enough to sense when the timing is off, when I am avoiding what I need to face, when I am putting aside the risk of failure by clicking through one more recipe.

I also know there are some food bloggers out there who click over to my place in order to avoid facing their own work and their potentially painful daily allotment of failure. We all have our unique shape of fear. There are no greener grasses, only different lawns. When it's hard to show up because I hate my calling, it helps me to rehearse what I know for sure—God has made me, God is remaking me, and God wants to come out of me in a unique way.

6. It's a waste of time. I can't say for sure, but I would guess this statement, more than any other, is one that isn't coming from your own head. You *know* your art is important. But someone else in your life has labeled it wasteful. *And you have believed them.*

The only reason we would ever call something a waste of time is because we have a certain idea of success and anything short of that idea we label "waste." Or maybe we are adhering to someone else's idea of success and we adopt it as our own.

If you are worried that your art is a waste of time, perhaps you need to redefine success in art.

Are you becoming more fully yourself?

Is there someone else who believes in you or has been inspired because you are living life more fully alive?

Are you learning what it means to depend on God in ways you've never had to depend on him before?

There is courage in connection—connection with your true self, with the true self of others, and with the one true God. If waking up to your desire is bringing you closer to someone else, if it allows you to be vulnerable in ways you weren't able to be before, if it reminds you of your desperate need for God, then your art has not been wasted.

Jesus shows himself through you in a million little ways. Perhaps more often than not, they are ways you can't plan for, don't intend, and may never even know about. There is no waste in the visible or invisible work of God.

7. It's too much work. Truer words have never been said. It takes work to show up, to be present, to engage your ideas and escort them with love and attention from seedling to full-grown, leafy, living art. But don't be fooled—it takes work to ignore it too. And that work can be just as painful, if not more so—running from the voice, hiding from inspiration, denying the way you were made, pretending you don't care about the art. Are you going to do the work of hiding or are you willing to show up and do the work of art?

8. Though I'm listing it last, this final statement could be the most powerful force keeping us from showing up. It is really more of a question, though I believe it sits in our heads like a dark fact: **Who do you think you are?**

When you finally show up, you will hear this question whisper dark words into your soul. When you are on the verge of discovery, on the edge of risk, when you're ready to take the next step toward influence—this question will come out of nowhere, asking *who do you think you are?*

After a lot of thought and effort to ignore it, I've come to realize the artist has to be willing to confront this question honestly, without blinking. Here are two actions to take when this question comes to mind:

Pay attention to what you're doing when you hear it. I bet you one million dollars you aren't watching TV. We have an enemy who wouldn't bother to threaten you if you weren't dangerous. So the question *who do you think you are?* only comes on the cusp of risk. Let that question become a signal to you: perhaps this work, this relationship, this dream, this effort has some life in it.

Steven Pressfield writes in his bestselling book *The War of Art,* "Self-doubt can be an ally. This is because it serves as an indicator of aspiration. It reflects love, love of something we dream of doing, and desire, desire to do it. If you find yourself asking yourself . . . 'Am I really a writer? Am I really an artist?' Chances are you are. The counterfeit innovator is wildly self-confident. The real one is scared to death."[3] The question *who do you think you are?* comes from a place of self-doubt. Instead of letting it silence you, force it to work for you.

The second action to take when this question comes to mind is this: *answer it.* Rather than push the question aside or crumble under the implications, demand that it be a reminder of your belovedness. Let it encourage you in your identity. Who *do* you think you are? Answer it. Here you have an opportunity to make art. Right now, in this moment, with the dark implications of that question still hot in your mind, decide that you will not let the art die here.

As you sit in the dark with your teenage son who came home after curfew for the third time this week, you are tired, angry, and don't have answers. The voice comes then, attacking your parenting: *Who do you think you are to parent this son well?*

Though you want to do anything other than show up in this moment—you have the authority to make a different choice. Make art with the way you love him, with the way you embrace your image-bearing identity, with the job you have been given to do. I don't know what you should say to him, but I do know you are the one to say it.

As you sit at your computer, staring blankly at an equally blank screen, you get a shred of an idea to write down. At first there is hope, but hope twists fast into doubt as the question whispers those foul six words into your soul: *Who do you think you are?*

Fight that question with answers before it has a chance to fester.

Who do you think you are? You are made in the image of Creator God and carry the presence of his Holy Spirit with you wherever you go.

You are a poem written inside the person of Christ and exist to carry out his inner desire. You are an image bearer and you have a job to do. Don't let that question derail you.

You are the beloved. So be the loved. Receive your beloved-ness and then hand it out, receive grace and be gracious to others, remember your image-bearing identity and move into the world with a job to do. Show up as you are with what you've been given. And don't allow the voice of doubt and discouragement to hold you back.

But doubt and discouragement aren't our only hindrances to showing up in the world. It is possible for us to uncover the art we were born to make and show up to release it into the world only to be met with silence, inability to make progress, and a seemingly impossible artless road ahead. The lack of movement isn't because of fear or sin or lack of belief. Sometimes it's simply God asking us to wait.

9

wait

It's not important who does the planting, or who does the watering. What's important is that God makes the seed grow.

—1 Corinthians 3:7

Much good happens in the space where nothing is happening.

—Christa Wells, *singer/songwriter*

I'm fifteen, sitting at home on a swaying piano bench. I play Debussy with great abandon, the haunting runs of "Clair de Lune" fill the room with translucent wonder, and I am certain there was never another more beautiful piece of music written anywhere in all the world.

The moon sings and "Clair de Lune" is what comes out.

And so at home, all the longings of my teenage heart pour out through my fingertips to the rhythm of these notes written by Debussy. I love to play the music.

But it's Wednesday afternoon and that means it's time for my piano lesson. I dread going because it's during my lesson that I actually hear what I sound like. Mrs. Weston listens to my first run through "Clair de Lune," her glasses sit far down her nose. Surely they'll fall off any minute. "How do you think you did on that?"

This is the worst kind of question.

I love to play piano. I loathe the scales and technique practice. Mrs. Weston can tell I haven't been practicing my scales just as sure as the dentist knows I never floss my teeth. I am the hunted, caught in her scope. I can't skip the hard parts or rush through the tricky finger placements in front of her. I can't pretend I sound good.

She reaches up and clicks on the metronome, the chain on the door of my musical heart. *Handcuffs*, I think, just as she lifts my slouching wrists to check my fingernails for length.

I can still hear that tick of the metronome, the heartbeat of the notes that bounce off hollow from the walls and the wood of the upright piano. *Just let me play how I want to!* But as I practice, that little ticking black box keeps my rhythm steady, reminds me to let the notes ring out in their full glory and give the rests their full stops.

Let the music say what it means to say in its complete musical phrase, then give it a chance to breathe before it speaks again.

The words of Rainer Maria Rilke come to mind: *"I am the rest between two notes."* We may spend whole seasons of our lives in this rest between the notes. All seems quiet, desolate even. We can't see the swelling of music rise up on either side of us—all we see and feel and know is this quiet nothing, this continual pause, this winter with white in all directions.

You are in a season of waiting. When you finally show up ready to release your art by being the person you believe you are created to be, there may be nothing more disheartening than to be asked to wait. The waiting can drive us mad if we let it. It can become a merciless dictator, shoving us into shapes we aren't made for, shapes of worry and doubt and short tempers.

But the waiting can also grow us, shape us from the inside out for sacred work. This is a kind of work that happens only in the secret place of abiding in the presence of Christ even in the midst of broken dreams and tired circumstance.

We have a Maker who doesn't just throw the sun up into the sky in a shock of fire, but pulls it up slow every morning and down the same way every night. And if you stare as it happens, the change is hard to see, but if you close your eyes and count to twenty, everything is different when you open them back up again. It's because a lot happens in the transition—secret things, beautiful things, Spirit-led things.

There is still movement in this waiting, though it may be hard to see.

Learning to Move While You Wait

John and I sit in the middle of a waiting season right now. He was in seminary when we got engaged, and two weeks after he graduated, we got married. As soon as we returned from our honeymoon, he began to work as a youth pastor.

That was twelve years ago. During these last two years, we've been sensing a change coming for us, but as we pray and talk and consider, we don't see what the change is. I ask him questions about what makes him come alive. *If you could do anything* kind of questions. His answers don't surprise me, but they do give new energy when he says them out loud. I can see the shape of his soul in some ways better than he can. I smile as I watch him begin to see it too.

We have asked the Lord to show us how to pray, and he has answered. He has not unveiled a vision for our lives that we can put into words yet. We can't write down a job description, point to a program or a particular ministry and say, *There. That is God's outline for our life.* He is speaking something different and has merely said two things:

Move toward God. In all things, see Jesus. In all circumstances, whether success or failure, questions or answers, beauty or ashes, acceptance or rejection, look for Jesus. When the girls are struggling through homework, when the dishwasher rack falls broken to the floor, when you sit in the midst of grief over losing a dad you love, look for Jesus. Stop trying so hard to read the Scriptures to look for answers but instead, let the Scriptures *read you.* Move toward God.

The second thing we sense God is saying to us is this: *Move toward one another.* In all things, love each other as you are but have a vision for what you could be. Pay attention to the vision God is casting for your marriage, your family, the community you live in. See one another according to the

Spirit, not according to the flesh. Move toward one another and receive the other as they move toward you.

We didn't know exactly what it meant to do these two things, moving toward God and toward each other. The simplest thing we could do, we did. In January of 2011, we began to pray together. Intentionally, willingly, desperately. It was a simple movement. Every morning, we woke a few minutes before the kids, grabbed a cup of coffee and one another's hands. Two minutes of prayer. That was it.

We listened quiet for answers. He offered love instead.

Our choice to pray was like an arrow in a bow. It took us in a direction we may not have walked in otherwise, like when an archer shifts ever so slightly to the left. The movement is small, but a hundred yards across the field, the arrow hits a vastly different mark. On that day, it didn't make much difference. But sitting here two years later, we are in a different place than we would have otherwise been.

We still don't have answers, at least not the kind we thought we wanted. But in the intentional time together, we are discovering something we want more than answers. I think God understands our desire for answers. I also believe, as I heard Dr. Crabb say once, that sometimes God withholds in his wisdom what he could provide by his power. I don't know why he does it, but I'm thankful I don't have to.

Instead of dreaming for big things in our future, I'm beginning to realize it's more important to dream *awake right now*. And so we wait. We move toward God because he first moved toward us, and we move toward one another in faith.

John often makes the statement, "Living things move." I don't know if, scientifically, that is completely true, but in my experience and from what I can see, that seems fairly accurate.

People move. Animals move. Plants move, although their movement is small and slow and gradual. But the roots burrow deep even when we can't see them. And the branches have everything they need for leaves even in the cold of winter. It simply isn't time for them to bloom.

Sometimes our living movement will be clear and swift: accept the job, marry the girl, move to Alaska, sing on the stage. Other times it will be so small it feels like stillness. But there is always movement in the waiting: walk to the kitchen, reach for his hand, close the eyes in wonder. In the waiting, there may be slowing, but there is never stopping. Not completely. Because living things move. God is always moving toward us and we always have the choice to move toward God. Even in the silence, even as we wait. Maybe especially so.

Learning to See While You Wait

It's Oprah, and she's talking to Steven Tyler on her show *The Next Chapter.* I'm oddly invested in this interview, interested in what she will ask, what he will say.

The next question: "Where do the songs come from? Are the songs always there, waiting to be uncovered? Or do they come in?"

I already know his answer. Even a forty-year rock icon knows better than to say his songs come from nothing, or even from himself. The best we can do is take God's imagination and re-imagine it new and in our own way. But we cannot make from nothing. *He is before all things, and in Him all things hold together* (Col. 1:17 NASB).

Steven answers. He says when he writes music, it is as if he is discovering something that is already there. He references Michelangelo, how he always saw David in the marble, but he just chiseled away the parts that weren't David.

> In every block of marble I see a statue as plain as though it stood before me, shaped and perfect in attitude and action. I have only to hew away the rough walls that imprison the lovely apparition to reveal it to the other eyes as mine see it.
>
> Michelangelo

The gift of the artist doesn't only rest in the hands that sculpt but in the eyes that see. Seeing the not-yet in the midst of the now is a perspective the artist has to carry. And so we ought to pray not only for *skill* but for *sight*.

An artist who sees reveals the shape of hope. As believers, we are seers and hopers. We listen hard for the healing and search long for the seeing of what could be in the midst of what is. We see the Davids in the stone.

Steven continues, says he grew up under the piano, listening to his dad play. So now, when he works on a song, "the melody's there, it's just waiting like a hanger, like a hat rack. And I'm waiting for the hat [to hang on it]."[1]

Artists see hat racks and we wait for hats. We know the words are there, the lyric, the image, the connection is possible—but waiting is a vital part of the creation process.

Michael Card, in his book *Scribbling in the Sand*, says when he writes a new song in the presence of God, "the words start to make more sense than anything I could have ever come up with on my own. They fit the melody like a glove, *as if the song was somehow preexistent and I am only just now hearing it*" (emphasis mine).[2]

As I write, I have the sense that this book exists but I haven't found it yet. I work, pray, labor, and squeeze out words. I take hands filled with hope and ideas, clasp them together, muddy. Sometimes what comes out is a mess. Other times, it fits like velvet on skin. Somehow, the whole process is art but it doesn't come from me. Not exactly, anyway.

I am uncovering it, a piece at a time. The work is finished somewhere invisible. My task is to uncover it, to find it—first in my imagination, then in tangible, holdable, sayable words.

Fear says I'm going the wrong way. Doubt says I won't find it at all. But hope? Hope says, *Wait. It's just a little farther. You are not alone and this is not just your idea.*

My goal is a finished book—I call that my art. Yet there is a deeper work happening. I chase what I think is the art, but really that's just the evidence. Like when I heard Sarah Masen sing that cold night in Michigan, her song was the evidence of a deeper work in her heart. The real art is the invisible work happening in the depths of my soul as I uncover, sink, see, listen, and wait.

The book is just the souvenir.[3]

There is a hope within you too, a desire longing for completion. It may not be a tangible work you can hold and point to. Your souvenir may be a relationship, an education, an investment, a charitable cause. As you stare at the stone of the hoped-for souvenir, remember the deeper work happening within you, where your life is hidden with Christ in God.

Learning to Trust While You Wait

We sit on the porch, arm to arm, hip to hip. The morning air is sharp, a cool blue breeze greets us from the left. I edge closer, press harder against him.

We remain still, looking straight ahead into the cul-de-sac, the round canvas of our lives. The kids are at school now, but I can still see them here in my mind, moving from Barbies on blankets to training wheels around the circle to whispered secret hideouts behind Ms. Jenny's bushes. A place usually filled with noise and chatter and neighborhood kids on our backyard trampoline, this morning is quiet.

We've been married nearly twelve years now and this one is the best yet. I know people say that a lot, but I really mean it. The dreaming and the waiting together has helped to wake us up to God and to one another. I consider the beauty of what we have and a bolt of fear strikes hard from nowhere, cracks the calm surface of contentment. *What if I lose him?*

Instead of an artist, I am a terrorist.

I sabotage the gift with my limited view of God's provision. If things are going as I would like, then God is good and can be trusted. But what if things go terribly wrong?

I am the walking terrified. I can move my mouth into shapes of worship and belief, but at the thought of losing, my mouth cups the questions. Remembering I don't have control does that, pushes me hard into fear. And fear reaches cold, dry hands down into my heart and twists into panic. We are asked to surrender to the invisible. *Lord, I believe. I beg for mercy in my unbelief.*

Each breath of this life is a mystery. But I don't have time for mystery. I want to solve it, define it, list it, explain it, dissect it, graph it, label it, and put it on a running ticker at the bottom of my screen so I can read it while I fold the towels.

I need to make the most of my time, you know.

In my flesh and in my fear, I need to prevent the mystery. When I do that, I may hold on to my illusion of control, but I simultaneously let go of the art.

God does things differently. He said, *Let there be light*, but then he waited a full day before he spoke again. And on the last day, he rested. He built waiting into creation. From the incarnation to the resurrection, divine creativity begins and ends with waiting.

God ushers in the mystery with a bright star and a host of angels. He gives mystery a name, said *Christ in you is the mystery*, and he invites us into a life of wonder. He has made the mystery known, but it has to be revealed. Revelation takes time, surrender, brokenness, and smallness.

The angel told Mary salvation would come through her body. For nine months, the Mystery grew within her in secret until that night in Bethlehem when he burst forth—the Poet becomes the *poiema*.

Mary's young body was transformed from the inside out, invisible God pouring out all over a stable floor. We paint her in pictures of glowing light, but it must have been dark and it must have been painful. There was blood and water before there was milk.

The shepherds heard the news and came to see the Messiah. Mary welcomed them in, remaining quiet in their presence. She considered these things in the depths of her heart, the implications for her, for her family, for the world. The baby was small but Mary knew the secret of this mystery.

Never despise the days of small beginnings.[4]

She opened herself wide to the world and God came out. She opened her heart wide to God and shut her mouth tight.

I don't like to shut my mouth, not when there's something I don't understand. Mysteries need solving and solving needs words and words come from my mouth and I can't make it stop. The artist is willing to shut her mouth and let God move in, through, around, *mysteriously*. She is willing to stick out her dirty feet and let God's love clean them.

He moves in this inner, upside-down, individual way and he places himself within us—those of us who, like Mary, say *yes*. He moves in our desires and then waters them, suns them, and sometimes dries them up. He always provides, but not always in the ways we think he ought to.

Consider the mystery of Christ in you. As soon as we ask for the how, we lose the wonder. The Spirit came over Mary in a moment, but it took nine months for him to grow. Jesus waited thirty years to begin what we call his earthly ministry. But really, wasn't he always being God in the world, from his first breath to his last? He was crucified and waited until day three to resurrect. Don't lose hope on day two.

Waiting paves the way for the art.

The Pain of Letting Things Grow

My three children finish their apples and get to the cores, find the seeds tiny and black inside. I watch as they talk without words to each other, eyes sparkling with what I know are visions of tall shade trees with bright red apples hanging low and sweet.

Rushing into the front yard in a blur of jackets and clenched hands, they scurry out to dig a hole in the grass. September air rushes through the door they leave open, and I watch as they cup small hands around that hole and witness the black seeds fall into their shallow plot of earth.

They cover those seeds and kneel beside the womb in the ground, waiting. And they water that mound in the middle of the front yard, draw a picture of an apple, tape it to a number two pencil, and stake it in the grassy dirt under dappled light.

Here is where we poured our hope and where we'll wait for it to grow. Every day after school, they run to that spot, spill the water, stand vigil to their imagination—faithful little servants to hope.

A few days pass and they become tired of the still mound. They want that ground to breathe, want to see life sprout up now, want to see how their labor gives way to newness.

Aren't we all seven years old, wanting our apple trees to give shade and fruit and wanting it yesterday? We kneel at the altar of our desire to see change now, to move things along, to push open doors. We have uncovered the art we were born to make and want to release the art we were made to live. We ignore the voice of fear and insecurity and are ready to move into our small world alive and awake.

Yet there seems to be only silence.

We don't want to wait.

And so because we can't see results, we decide it isn't working.

Did my great-grandfather Pop think those kinds of thoughts as he watched his son's New York City career slip slow into the amber hands of the Miller Lite?

Did he wonder if those short trips to Florida with his grand-son, my dad, would ever make a difference in the scope of things?

Did he worry about the future of his children's children because how could a family brought up under the instruction of alcohol ever make anything of themselves?

Pop died before he saw the impact of his love and intention. Would he ever have believed that my dad stopped drinking and my grandpa did too? We benefit from the faithful artists and influencers who came before us. They did not live to see the change, but we live because of it.

Be faithful to plant. Release the growing to God. Open up clenched fists and let the seeds drop into the ground, let them burrow down deep and do their secret work in the dark. Sacred shaping happens in the waiting. In the words of Sir Henry John Newbold, "Let us build for the years we shall not see."

I join my sister in the kitchen to mix the flour and salt and water together for the bread. But I miscount and it looks like the bread won't rise after all.

Things like this don't work out for me. I'll never try this again. I say it out loud and she tries to encourage. I feel the sinking soul, how a small thing like wrongly measured flour can rub so heavy against deep insecurity.

Where does this creeping darkness come from? How can so little a thing grab my ankles and spiral me down?

My eyes rest long on the second things of life, things like outcomes, measurable impact, and my own self-confidence or rather the lack of it. I'm sinking into a death of my own doing, I lose sight of what I know for sure.

I want to make the dough with my own hands, but my hands make mistakes and I hate my own failures. I don't see results, so instead of waiting in faith I curse the art altogether. *This is a waste of my time.*

We don't like to waste our time. The mere idea of "wasting time" is laughable, really. If the dictionary is right and *waste* means "an act or instance of using or expending something carelessly, extravagantly, or to no purpose."

And if *time* is "the continued progress of existence," then could *wasting time* be translated as "extravagantly existing"? Might it be worth the risk?

We put the dough aside anyway, figure we've nothing to lose in letting it sit there on the counter. Maybe time will do her work. I may have added these ingredients together, but I can't make them breathe anyway, even if I mixed them up right. The idea that I could make dough with my own hands turns laughable now. *Really? Where do you keep your storehouses of water? Did you mine the rocks or capture the seawater to get that salt?*

I am a student of bread and of life. Maybe I'm not as in control as I like to believe. Maybe the art isn't about me.

The minutes pass and we are distracted with the kids and some conversation. We chat as I clean up the counter, carry the sack of flour across the kitchen where it lives on the top shelf. My sister laughs behind me, points to the spot where the failing dough sat. My eyes follow her gaze and I feel a smile fill my face right up.

Not only is the dough rising, it's flowing over the top of the plastic container. It rises up so high it falls right out, and my hope swells right along with it. I cup my hands over the warm dough, brush flour from the top onto the cornmeal-covered pizza peel.

When water and yeast meet flour and salt and *time*, they rise up together, mingling in the bowl so we can't tell one from the other. They make a new thing in spite of my miscounting. They just needed time to mingle.

When I put the loaf in the oven, the heavy dough sits rounded on the stone. As it begins to move, I watch in wonder. We eat the bread for dinner, topped thick with butter mixed with honey from the farmers' market.

Sacred and secret things happen in the waiting. Moments of heaven touch earth, breathe life into babies inside their mamas and bread sitting on my counter. The work is invisible, but the result is not.

As I watch that bread breathe, that's when I feel it—the quiet lifting that comes from accepting the secret things of the mystery. *So this is courage.* The waiting and movement come first, and the courage follows close on the heels of art.

Show up in the place where you already are fully alive as the image bearer God made you to be. Embrace the mysterious, invisible work of Christ even when it seems like nothing is happening. You are an image bearer and you have a job to do—whether you see the results or whether you don't.

10

offer

Our gifts are not from God to us, but from God through us to the world.

—Janice Elsheimer, *The Creative Call*

The preschool hallway at church is crowded with high-heeled women and slack-wearing men. The girls hold on to various parts of my coat while I navigate my way to my son's classroom. As we pass the window looking into the two-year-old room, an out-of-place image in the corner catches my eye. A man stands still, children scurry around him on knees and Play-Doh–covered hands.

He holds a violin in rest position.

I stop in the middle of the hallway, move off to the side with my caravan of three, fascinated by the odd scene on the other side of the window. We stay there and watch as this suited-man lifts the violin from beneath his arm, pauses for a moment, and begins to play. Thick ribbons of blue and deep green fill the nursery as the children carry on with their usual tasks—stacking blocks, sorting oversized Legos, babbling. His music is passionate and full.

This man is not a student trying to earn credits or an intern filling his time sheet. He is a full-fledged professional. I am ashamed to tell you my first thought: *What a waste of that beautiful music.*

In that moment, my ideas about art and art-making were limited. I believed somehow the effort of the artist depended upon the appreciation of the audience.

Offer Whatever You Have

In John 2, I read about the couple who invited Jesus to their wedding. They chose him, his disciples and his mama too. I wonder what kind of friend he was. Did he cry when they made their promises? Did he and the groom shake hands, exchange looks, or embrace? What did he think as he watched the bride? Did he think of his church? Of me? Of you?

When I hoard my gifts and my gifting under piles of doubt, perfectionism, and demand for appreciation, I forget the six pots in Cana filled with dusty water, the ones holding nearly thirty gallons each. If I'm a violin player and I reason myself out of playing for these little ones because they won't appreciate it or because that work is beneath me, I forget how Jesus takes small offerings and turns them around to glorify his Father. I forget the secret way he did his work and the twinkle in Mary's eyes when she told the servants, "Do whatever he tells you."

I also forget the miracle worked invisibly inside those stone pots and the satisfaction from the master of the banquet when the rich wine graced his lips. It was only a wedding. Doesn't the King of the Universe want to pick a grander stage to debut his first miracle? Only his mother and a handful of servants knew about it. He didn't save a life or offer world peace or end starvation or prevent anything dangerous at all.

Jesus worked a secret miracle to satisfy guests at a wedding and to keep a host from embarrassment. He did not wait for a bigger spotlight. He did not make any announcements. He did not hand out a brochure with his bio and credentials.

Blessed are those who bring him their small cups of water. Blessed are those who bring big stone pots too. He does miracle things with the offering no matter what it is.

I am desperate for a life filled with twinkling eyes, for thirty-gallon water pots, for believing in things I can't see, for cups filled with secret miracles.

Offer Regardless of Outcomes

I don't know what your gifts are, but I know they carry hints of how you are made, who you were made to be, your own personal reflection of the image of God. Depending on the vocational art you practice, there may be a place to market, promote, sell, and professionalize your art. The artist may need to manage her art. But if she begins to feel compelled to ration it, to hoard and hold her art tightly in both hands, it might be time to sink into God again. It might be time to be still, to break the alabaster jar that holds her sweet-smelling gift and release the art back into the hands of God.

When it comes to the kind of art we make as our vocation, if it is at all possible, be generous with your gifts. Be fully who you are in the presence of others. You are not asked to manage outcomes. You are simply asked to come out.

This may mean we have to change our mind about scarcity. The world says if I give my art away to you, then I don't have it anymore. The world tells me to hold on, to protect my valuable gifts and treat them as property.

In John 6, you can read the familiar story of Jesus feeding the five thousand with just a few fish and loaves of bread from a young boy. The scene I typically imagine is a boy with a lunch his mama packed for him. And that may have been the case. But it's also likely this was an older boy with a job to do. This changes the scene a little.

Some theologians believe the five loaves and two fish represented not just a lunch but a livelihood.[1] Young boys were given permission to sell food wherever large groups of people gathered. That day by the sea when Jesus taught, there were at least five thousand men. Business was sure to be good. This bread was probably made with barley, a grain cheaper than wheat and used by poorer people to make bread. This boy had a job to do and not many resources with which to do it.

Imagine what may have been going through his mind when Andrew walked over to him and asked for his scant amount of loaves and fish. Perhaps the boy was excited, thinking he was sure to sell it all now that this friend of Jesus had pointed him out. Or maybe there was fear. *Is this man going to pay me for the food he's taking? Or does he plan to* [gasp] *give it away?!*

The Bible doesn't say what was going on in the young boy's mind. But it does say Jesus took the loaves, gave thanks, and distributed them to the people. He did the same thing with the fish until all the people had as much as they wanted.

Whether water and wine or bread and fish, Jesus is present to the people, right where they are in the midst of their needs. Jesus doesn't *reflect* the image of God, he *is* God. He moves to the rhythm of the Spirit of God, takes water and transforms it into wine. He receives a meager offering of bread and fish, blesses it, and hands it out in abundance. He takes small offerings and remakes them for the good of people to the glory of his Father.

As you move to the rhythm of the Spirit of God, what is within you that you can now give to someone else? Not for the glory of yourself, but as a person who bears the image of God in the world. What are those things in the deepest part of who you are, the personality and desires and unique blending of history and circumstance and longing—what is most alive in you as you are united with Christ that you can now pour out as an offering unto God for the benefit of others?

No matter how small, how weak, how meager. No matter what skill or training or lack. That's what it means to uncover the art you were born to make and release the art you were made to live.

It isn't about you finding those things that make you come alive so that you will be awesome and admired. It isn't about discovering the art you were born to make because that is the highest goal of humanity. It isn't about getting in touch with your desires so that you can forsake all responsibility and obligation and do what you want because you deserve it. It isn't about becoming famous. It is about becoming *yourself.*

This uncovering and releasing is most deeply about discovering how the shape of your soul is at odds with God without Jesus, but through Christ you have been made a friend. And because you are now a friend, a child, the beloved of God, you have a job to do. That job may take on many different forms and many different descriptions during your lifetime, and it won't always be enjoyable.

But you, as an image-bearing poem, are called by God to offer yourself alive in the world, for his glory and for the benefit of others. You are God's workmanship created in Christ to do good works, to carry out the inner desire of Jesus, to make art with your life.

And this is what you most deeply want. If you believe that your desires can be satisfied outside of Jesus Christ, then releasing the art you were made to live will be irrelevant to you. You will go off chasing lesser things, living a second-things life, trying to turn water to wine on your own for the sake of the wine and not to the glory of God.

Let this bread and wine miracle lead you to something deeper.

He tells us to take the bread and to take the wine and eat and drink to remember his body, broken for us; his blood, spilled on our behalf. There was bread and wine on earth to meet the needs of needy people. There is bread and wine in the Spirit to do the same. God is the one who offers. All we can do is take what he has given to us and offer it back to him in the form of giving it away to others. Our offerings aren't efforts worked up inside ourselves. Our offerings are unique responses to a living, giving God.

As you take the bread and wine from Jesus, you offer it to others. It is not your job to make them receive it in a certain way or with a certain amount of appreciation. It is only your job to offer it.

Live your life like a hostess who serves the people at her table. She looks them in the eye, meets them where they are. She doesn't spend her time distracted during the party, hiding out in the next room, calling all the people who said they couldn't come. She doesn't try to please a group who has already said "No thank you" rather than serve the guests who want more.

Issue the invitation. Serve those who show up with what you have and who you are by offering yourself and receiving the offering they bring as well.

This is the church, congruent with Ephesians 4:15–16, that essentially says the body grows when all its members give what they have to give—"we will speak the truth in love, growing in every way more and more like Christ, who is the head of his body, the church. He makes the whole body fit together perfectly. As each part does its own special work, it helps the other parts grow, so that the whole body is healthy and growing and full of love."

Offer Your Weakness

To encourage you to offer your weakness perhaps implies that everything before this wasn't from weakness. But here I want to speak directly to it. As I write this book, I am desperately aware of how far I am from living these words fully. The words of Henri Nouwen resonate deeply within me:

Sometimes we are called to proclaim God's love even when we are not yet fully able to live it. Does that mean we are hypocrites? Only when our own words no longer call us to conversion. Nobody completely lives up to his or her own ideals and visions. But by proclaiming our ideals and visions with great conviction and great humility, we may gradually grow into the truth we speak. As long as we know that our lives always will speak louder than our words, we can trust that our words will remain humble.[2]

One of my deepest internal struggles, one of the reasons I nearly chose not to write at all, is because living life in the Spirit the way I want to write about it takes courage that I don't have. Some days I wonder if I'm making it all up. Other days my ugliness far outweighs my attraction and my flesh wins only to win again.

Knowing we can't fully live the words we call others to live can keep us from ever saying the words at all. The same goes for any kind of art we make. How can I encourage you to release the art you were made to live if I so desperately struggle to do that myself?

I write about uncovering your art and releasing it into the world. I write about courage and embracing your deepest identity. But in the next breath, I get scared and quiet. I have big doubts and bigger procrastination tactics. The critics whisper and roar and I run from them, mostly the ones in my head. What could I possibly have to say? I'm not an artist. I'm making this stuff up, right?

I'm asking people to live a life I can't fully live myself, and that feels unacceptable. But when I get quiet and consider my lack in the presence of God, I know this is what I have to offer, for better or worse. The art I believe I was born to make lingers even in the midst of my inadequacy.

Just because you can't fully live your life the way you so long to live it doesn't mean you don't fully believe it's possible with all your heart. And it doesn't mean you are forbidden to share what you're learning unless you are living it perfectly.

Christ is in you and wants to come out through you in a million little ways—through your strength and also your weakness, your abilities and also your lack.

I call it art, someone else calls it rubbish.

So what?

Call it what you will. God calls us his poem. And the job of the poem is to inspire. To sing. To express the full spectrum of the human experience—both the bright hope that comes with victory and the profound loss that accompanies defeat.

We must make art, even in our weakness. If we don't, we are denying ourselves *ourselves*. In turn, we will deny everyone else ourselves as well.

My dad, the alcoholic blue-collar–worker-turned-sober, believing, professional communicator, says this:

> I'm slow, not prolific. I have to think and concentrate to get anything done. I'm disorganized and messy. I speak when I should shut up and shut up when I should speak. I talk too loud and too long. And my head's shaped like a light bulb. Just because I don't like something about myself doesn't mean it's sin. Sometimes I worry more over those parts than the parts that are sin. Isn't there enough of the sin to worry about without micro-managing the unique aspects of your personality? If who you are is random, then yeah, go on a self-improvement program. But if you think God is in control

of the whole thing of you, and he made you on purpose for a reason, and you try to be someone else, who will be you?[3]

Some stuff about us are faults or sin or change-worthy. But I think a lot of those things we try to make different are actually the things that *make us different*. It can all be an offering. Part of the art is having the faith to believe that Jesus still works miracles, even in our weakness. Maybe especially so.

Offer Your Brave Yes and Your Strong No

When you consider what it means for you to release the art you were made to live into the world, it can be easy to begin to believe that saying yes is godly and saying no is selfish. *Say yes to God*, the believers say. *This is your offering*. But what does that even mean?

When John proposed that warm day in early September, I said yes (of course) and that one word propelled us forward into the next part of our lives together. I still say yes to us every day. No one asks if I will take this man every morning when I get up. But I do take him, whether the day is worse or better. He asked the question once. I answer him with my life.

If things go wrong or life gets crazy, it doesn't mean I should have said no. It just means the world is broken and we still live in it. And so the success of our yes does not depend upon our circumstance but upon our convictions. We usually know this is true in marriage, but it's true in other things too.

Saying yes to my marriage with my life is saying yes to God. Showing up where I am and not where I wish I were is saying yes to God. Listening to a friend share her struggles without trying to fix her is saying yes to God. We offer our yeses to one another with the ways we move and serve and love among people, and in so doing, we are saying yes to God and making art with our lives.

Yes requires something of me. Movement. Commitment. Sacrifice. We know saying yes means a lot, implies a lot. We are tempted to hide behind no and leave the yeses for the brave and the courageous—those who are not us.

But your world would be different if you were not in it. And your brave yes might be just what we're waiting for. *Yes, I will believe, I will move, I will open my eyes, I will show up.* You might not like what you see. You might be afraid of what is required of you. But yes is the first step and you are not alone. You are not asked to manage the outcome or ensure the success. Sometimes you are simply invited to show up and say yes.

But saying yes is not the only way to offer ourselves to God. Sometimes making art in the world means taking the risk to move toward a goal or a person, knowing you could fail but facing it anyway. Other times, the art we are to make in the world comes as a result of saying no and staying seated even when it seems like we should stand.

For every brave yes, there is often a no that comes right along with it. To say no could be just as artful a response as saying yes ever was.

We have to be confident enough in our decisions that a narrowed eye from a fellow parent doesn't sway us, that pressure from a leader at church doesn't force our hand, that a harsh but well-intended word from a relative doesn't derail our priorities. Don't let the easily offended critic set the agenda. Believe in your yes. Hold fast to your no.

People may love you, respect you, look up to you, want to be with you, *but they will not say no for you.* They will let you work and volunteer as long as you are willing. They will let you lead and be strong and move ahead if you want to. Don't get mad at them for letting you continue to say yes. Only you know your boundaries. If you don't, might I encourage you to find them out? Because yes can be brave, but it can also be bossy. It can become an addiction. Before you realize it, all of your yeses are to obligation and duty. And because of those obligated yeses, you are forced to look passion and intention and desire in the eye and say, *No, I don't have time for you.* Weigh the cost your yes will have on your spirit, your soul, and your body. You may have to search for your brave yes, *but you will have to fight for your strong no.*

One reason why it is important to uncover the art alive within us is it helps us to discern our yes from our no. There is no formula to discovering when to say which one. There is only Jesus, doing as he sees his Father do, asking us to do as he does. Love God. Love people. This may look different for you than it does for me. This may look different for you today than it did for you last year. That's because you are a poem, not a robot.

Remember the rhythm you were born to move with. As you sink into God, as he gives you eyes to see, as you continue to show up where you are, you will be able to offer your brave yes and your strong no with confidence and conviction.

Life is art. And art demands creativity; it cannot tolerate formulas. Building a good marriage is art. Handling relational conflict is art. Trusting God with your sexual addiction or depression or fear of disapproval is art. God doesn't provide

171

recipes to cook up a delicious life *because He can't*. Machines aren't beautiful; waterfalls are. We're not machines. We're more like waterfalls, waterfalls who are persons.[4]

Larry Crabb, *Real Church*

Offer Your Art in the Presence of Another

If you hadn't already guessed it, my future in piano playing was short-lived. At first I tried to make it work and even chose piano as my major when I went off to college. I joined a traveling group of singers as their accompanist as a freshman, playing in churches and at recitals on campus.

Still, I never particularly looked forward to playing piano in front of people. I was uncomfortable sharing that part of my art in the presence of others. During Christmas break, when Dad asked me to play for family gatherings, I tried to get out of it. Before performances with this traveling group, I got so nervous my hands shook and I worried I would be unable to turn the pages of my sheet music.

After two years of struggling through required practice, theory classes, and metronomes, I decided to quit. The constant nerves and anxiety associated with performing combined with the hours of solitude in tiny fluorescent-lit rooms with Chopin and Czerny weren't worth the outcome anymore. I quit because I wanted to love it again. The joy of the art of piano playing didn't outweigh the responsibility enough for me to stick with it. It didn't matter to me if I shared it or not. Playing in an empty room felt more like worship than doing it in the presence of others ever did. I wanted to keep it that way.

Writing, on the other hand, is entirely different. For a long time, writing was private for me. During high school, I started writing my journal on my dad's desktop computer, mainly because I had so much I wanted to say that my hand couldn't keep up with my heart. I typed out words fast in that journal, and then I printed out each entry, slid the pages into plastic protectors, and collected them all in a two-inch binder.

I took that binder to college with me even though I didn't own a computer. Whenever I felt particularly brave, I headed to the computer lab next to the library on campus and typed a little something to add to my binder. It was terrifying work because the lab was always filled with other students. I would open a new document, type out my heart, hit print, and then run across the room to stand guard at the printer before anyone else picked up my guts by accident. Once I had the copy safely in hand, I would rush back to the computer where I was working and swiftly deleted all evidence that I had ever come alive at all. *Print out desire for safekeeping but, for the love of humanity, don't let anyone see.*

One time during a conversation with my roommate Faith, I was trying to explain to her a particular perspective I had on something but I couldn't find the words to say it out loud. So I pulled out my binder from under my twin bed and began flipping through the glossy pages. I can't imagine what it must have looked like from her perspective, a thick notebook filled with single-spaced words. But I knew my way around that journal and quickly found what I was looking for. I trusted her enough by that time to read to her a portion that said what I wanted her to know.

She kindly listened, watched me as I talked. She flung herself across my bed, propped up on an elbow, sock feet hanging off the side. She responded, not to what I read, but to the fact that I wrote it at all. "When you write all that stuff, do you write like you expect someone's going to read it one day?"

Her question surprised me. I didn't write to be read, I wrote because I loved to write. But there *was* always a vague sense of a reader, even though the mere idea of someone reading what I wrote in that journal terrified me. I was comfortable enough with her to offer a sliver of my authentic self, but not the whole. Still, her question made me think.

The song from Sunday school about letting our light shine comes to mind: "Hide it under a bushel, no! I'm gonna let it shine." The song is based on Matthew 5:16—"Let your light shine before men in such a way that they may see your good works, and glorify your Father who is in heaven" (NASB). I know the light is Jesus, but where does the light come out, exactly? Through my facial expressions? My words? My hands? How I dress?

I don't know what Harry Dixon Leos imagined when he penned the song, but I do know what Matthew 5:16 implies. This phrase for "good works" is the same one used in Ephesians 2:10—"For we are His workmanship, created in Christ Jesus for good works" (NASB). This is the good work prepared for us in advance, the good work that carries out the inner desire of Christ, the work of his *poiema*.

As image bearers with a job to do, what else would be our offering than the work God has prepared us to do? And how else would we offer it than by sharing who we most deeply are in the presence of others?

174

As you embrace your unique image-bearing identity, you are becoming more fully yourself. That means you have an awareness of what is most alive within you and can now offer it up to God. But this is not a vague and untouchable offering.

Think of Mary who told the servants to bring the water pots to Jesus, and Jesus transformed the offering into something that blessed the wedding guests. Think of the young boy on the hillside who, through the prompting of Andrew, offered the loaves and fishes to Jesus. Again, Jesus transformed the offering into something that blessed and nourished the crowd. People bring simple offerings to Jesus, and then Jesus hands miracles back to the people. Neither of these were vague or invisible offerings "up to God." They required real movement on earth toward the person of Jesus.

And now the person of Jesus lives in people like you.

As I now write, I offer my words to you. In so doing, I am offering them to Jesus. It's the same with any kind of art we make on earth, whether it be the work of skilled hands, an open heart, listening ears, a hope-filled vision. Our offerings aren't vague and invisible. Our specific offerings reveal the unique version of our worship, not for the glory of us, but to the glory of God and for the benefit of others.

We commit ourselves to Him, yes; but far more important, He has committed Himself to us, and what He takes He holds, and what He holds He moulds, and what He moulds He uses. So we launch out into the deep of God. We launch out by recognizing that He has already seized hold of us and launched us out in His beloved Son, in whom we are and He in us.[5]

Norman Grubb, *The Spontaneous You*

11

wonder

Wonder is the only adequate launching pad for exploring a spirituality of creation, keeping us open-eyed, expectant, alive to life that is always more than we can account for, that always exceeds our calculation, that is always beyond anything we can make.[1]

—Eugene Peterson

The more I think about that violinist in the church nursery, the more I change my mind about him. Not only do I see him as generous with his art, offering himself as himself in a way only he could do, but his violin music was a perfect theme song for the nursery.

Wonder is normal for these little ones. The violinist is just as wonderful as the ball in the corner. They are unimpressed by his professional music because everything is equally impressive in their world. Peekaboo is as interesting as a Picasso. Their right hand is endlessly fascinating. All those moving fingers!

They haven't yet learned to categorize their appreciation of art into worth and waste. The violin music was a perfectly normal backdrop to their perfectly wonderful world.

A child sees the wonder, takes it in, picks it up, and walks among it. A rock, a leaf, a giraffe, a violinist—it is all wonderful to him. He plays an air guitar, draws a picture of a tree, traces his hand on a piece of blue paper. Why not?

The ease with which I am able to release the art I was made to live seems directly related to my willingness to embrace wonder.

The Wonder of Union

The violinist in the nursery has the unique talent of playing the violin and that is a wonder all by itself. But consider his two legs holding him up, his two hands moving the bow, and his lungs breathing in the air around his head—this is a deeper wonder, still.

It's a wonder he can play the violin.

It's a greater wonder he can *hold* a violin.

Perhaps most wonderful of all of these is that his breathing, standing, and violining all point to a God who does all those things as well, a God who is *with us* through his union with this violinist. In a very real sense, God stands in the corner of

177

the nursery and holds a violin. God shows himself through the poetry of the man's work and the art of the man's life.

God reveals a bit of his own glory through the unique personality, talents, choices, and desires of the artist. And as this violin man pours out what is most alive in him through his music, it touches a place deep inside of me.

It isn't better for an artist to play for free for a group of toddlers than it is for him to play for money at Carnegie Hall. The point isn't which is better or which is more holy or pleasing to God. The point instead is to be alive in the presence of Jesus no matter who you're with, what you're doing, what's gone wrong, or how much (or how little) you are paid.

I sit with a group of new friends for dinner around a table. The quietest among us asks question after question, looks deeply into the eyes of each one talking. Finally someone directs the questions back toward him. "You are so intentional with your questions. What compels you to ask and to honestly seek the answers?"

I have to lean forward to hear his soft voice. His answer is slow but intentional. "I know Christ more as he comes out of you than in my own imagination."

He seeks to know people because it is through people that Christ reveals himself.

He spoke truth when he said to the circle of us around the table, *I experience God through you more fully than I can without you.* This is the greatest wonder, not only that God can show himself through us, but that he *prefers* it.

Christ in you, *as you.* Christ, clothed in your humanity. Christ, with all of your talents and weaknesses and natural inclinations. Christ coming out through your unique personality. Christ serving them lunch, washing their clothes, making a meal for a neighbor. Not to say that you are Christ, but that he has chosen you, as you are and not as you wish you were, he has chosen you to live within.

Christ, playing the violin.

He invites you to move with the rhythm of his Spirit. This is a mystery and wonder that is the gospel. He doesn't wait until we are conformed to a version of ourselves that we are pleased with. He comes in and transforms us from the inside out.

The Wonder of Life on the Earth

Life can be carried only in the hands of the unhurried.[2]

Ann Voskamp, *One Thousand Gifts*

He carries the umbrella with him up the tree, not a rain cloud in sight. Why does he do it? Because he can, I guess. I worry he'll lose his balance and won't have free hands to catch himself.

He doesn't think of falling, he thinks only of floating.

I have him leave the umbrella behind. It's time to pick up the girls from their after-school activities. What practical use is there for an umbrella on a sunny day?

We do this every afternoon. And most of the time, I hear myself telling him, "Hurry up, we're gonna be late. We don't want to keep the girls waiting." And his legs, growing for only a little over five years, quicken for a few steps. But then he sees a stick or a pointy leaf and must stop to touch, to pick up, to handle the wonder.

They're like magnets, his little hands to nature. In a stroke of brilliance, I think, *Hmm. Perhaps I should leave ten minutes earlier. Maybe I should consider scheduling in time for the wonder.* So we do. We leave early, we walk slowly, we stay silent, we stop. It is all a part of the plan, and so we are sure not to miss it.

Sarah Young's words come to mind: *Hurry keeps the heart earthbound.* If she's right, then perhaps slow escorts the heart to heaven.

Sometimes I'm home, but I'm not always here. I have to fight to stay in the moment. I fight the pull of the list, the email, the laundry, the window-staring. I look at the clock and promise myself, *For the next twenty minutes, I will sit here without getting up. And I will play cars.* When did play become such hard work? I never imagined that I would have to fight to keep the wonder.

But fight, I do. It's a messy fight, not at all consistent. I try not to dwell on my lack and the shame that sometimes threatens to overwhelm. Instead, I think about the wonder, about this moment, and about the God who gives good gifts. Thankfulness can chase away a thousand thoughts of shame.

The smallest and tiniest gifts take us by the hand to reveal the greatest and most holy truths. That these small gifts can point so undeniably to the greatest Giver is a wonder all by itself.

But we can't ignore the Big Problem with the wonder of life on earth.

N. D. Wilson narrows down the problem into two parts. "Part One," he writes in his book, *Notes from the Tilt-A-Whirl*, ". . . Eyelashes exist, and my daughters' are curly. They love to brush them on my cheeks, and that fleeting touch, that dragging whisper, is more real than your heroin dreams."[3] In other words, cute things exist and the world is packed with beauty.

The problem, Part Two? "The world is rated R, and no one is checking IDs. Do not try to make it G by imagining the shadows away. Do not try to hide your children from the world forever, but do not pretend there is no danger. Train them. Give them sharp eyes and bellies full of laughter. Make them dangerous. Make them yeast and when they've grown, they will pollute the shadows."[4]

We don't embrace the wonder of life on earth by calling the bad things good. The bad things are bad. Cancer steals. People make horrible decisions. Children are abandoned. There really is abuse, injustice, dysfunction, and war. Jesus really was crucified.

The hope of all believers is that, in the end, the good wins out. The death of Christ was horrific. But the victory of his resurrection was more wonderful than the terror of his crucifixion. Living life like an artist means seeing both sides and knowing who wins.

The Wonder of Time on Earth

November night comes on strong. Gone are the days of October's hints, trees dressed in colorful coats, teasing cool and playful dance. November comes in with her collar up, scarf tucked in tight. She opens her arms to the wind, releases her leaves to the ground.

It's a hot chocolate kind of night, but we're out of the packets so I prepare to leave for the neighborhood store.

Walking fast to my car, I know I won't stop shaking for at least five minutes. The seat seeps cold through my corduroys, I grab the steering wheel and back out of the driveway. That's when the snow starts to fall.

The excitement of flurries distracts me. It's North Carolina so we get snow most every winter, but not often before December. When I get home, I realize in all the excitement I accidentally bought the mocha cappuccino kind of packets instead of the regular kind with the mini marshmallows. Serving coffee to snow-crazy kids doesn't seem like a good idea.

So instead, I pull out the Hershey's cocoa and make the recipe on the tin with the dash of salt and bit of vanilla. I should have done this in the first place.

I don't know if it is the snow falling fast or the peppermint sticks I bought for eighty-seven cents, but it is the best cup of chocolate I think I've ever had. Definitely the best I've ever made. Or maybe it's the fact that I didn't expect it to snow anyway and the whole day is a blessed gift.

If I think about all the happiest days of my life so far, all the spectacular ones come to mind. Our wedding day was happy because of what it represented, but I tend to use words like *sacred* and *important* for that day instead. It was happy, but also stressful.

The day the twins were born was miraculous and joyous, but I weighed nearly as much as my six-foot-two-inch husband and they came out way too early. There was lots of fear and tears and worry weaving itself through that happy day.

We've had a lot of great vacations together, from our honeymoon trip to Maine when we were wide-eyed and sun-kissed, to our family trip to Disney last year when every moment was magic . . . -ish. But those were so built up, so planned for and expensive, it was hard to simply go with the flow when the flow wasn't on the schedule.

And then a memory came to mind when I was pregnant with the twins, but we didn't yet know they were twins. John and I went in for a routine appointment to hear the baby's heartbeat, and the edges of our nervous excitement quickly turned jagged when the nurse said she couldn't find one. We walked foggy-like into the dark ultrasound room and waited.

Scenarios sped through my mind on a fast-forward movie reel. I planned for a miscarriage, for a heart defect, for a great disappointment, for a loss. My mind didn't naturally gravitate toward hope.

When the doctor put that cold wand on my tummy, peered close to the screen, and turned it our way, she calmly said to us, "Well, you aren't eleven weeks after all. You're only seven. And there's two."

Two what?

"Two babies. You're having twins! Congratulations!"

Nurses gathered in the hallway to look in on us as I had visions of two car seats and matching outfits and John couldn't stop laughing.

Somehow we made it from the exam room to the car when we realized, *twins*. And the best part was yet to come, because now we got to tell everyone. We've never had so much fun. It was one of the purest, happiest days in all my life. Terrifying, but only vaguely. I never expected it in a thousand years.

That's part of what makes most of the happy days happy. Unexpected gifts. Snow before Christmas. Hot chocolate with vanilla. Telling the family, "There's two!"

I know there's a time for everything, but it's easier to accept the wonder of the beginnings and the daily gifts than for the endings and the daily struggles. I am more eager to embrace the time for birth than the time for death.

As Frank entered the last weeks of his appointed time, there was sadness in the knowing. But aren't we all approaching that time, living one day closer to our last? He may get there first, but we'll all get there eventually. Everyone is living a story, and we watched as his came to an end. As it did, we began to count the gifts with every word spoken. When someone says *I love you* when they're dying, it seems to mean more than in the middle of their living.

But why? Perhaps because we've forgotten how to embrace the wonder of time on earth. The sweetness of those words gets lost in the busy, and it's only here at the end where we pause long enough to realize how heavy they are with grace and blessing. We try to pack more meaning in the ends and beginnings, but I wonder if the Lord sees them all the same?

A daughter's moment of birth bursts with the same amount of blessings as a Thursday afternoon six years later when she comes home from school and plops her bag on the floor. Isn't the day we said *I do* filled with the same kind of wonder as ten years later when we pass the beans and biscuits around our Kmart table? Isn't the 22nd day of kindergarten equally as monumental as the first and 76th day and the last? Because in each of those days, we *live* and *move* and are.

Eternity is not for later.

God weaves eternity into our minutes. Every day, he is creating minute after minute, and he hands us the grace we need for each one as they come. Worry and anxiety show up when we try to rush ahead into the minutes that haven't been made yet. There is no art in anxiety. We try to manage the future, a time that doesn't even exist yet, and we wonder why it makes our stomach hurt.

When we stepped off the elevator for the first time on the Palliative Care Unit to visit Frank, I had the distinct feeling of the presence of God. *This is a place where heaven touches earth.* It was real, palpable, comforting. But heaven touches earth in my living room too. In my bedroom and in my front yard and on top of the Empire State Building and on an island in the middle of the sea and in the cardboard houses in Manila and on my front porch. Heaven touches earth every minute, when I touch my husband's hand and look into his eyes, when the girls whisper good nights and I love yous and the boy makes a mess with toy airplanes and crayons. Heaven is touching earth right now. But sometimes it takes endings for us to see it.

Every artist knows the struggle in beginning, in finally taking the time to move into beauty in a way that will shape and design what *is* into something that *hasn't yet been*. But as difficult as it is to start, it could be equally as difficult to say that you are finished. I want to hold on to the loose ends. I want the freedom to make it better. I want to manage outcomes and to ensure that all will be well with me and those whom I love. I want to hold on to the endings.

The finishing up of anything requires a great deal more resolve than we had to dig for in the beginning. But we are told that our times are in the hands of God, that we are loved everlasting, and that he has already made all things well with us. There is great comfort there, and I keep coming back to that.

Sometimes the doctor says, "It's twins!" Another time, he says, "It's cancer." There is a wonder to the boundaries of time on earth—a terrible, fantastic, mysterious wonder. Trees and ground and garden are bursting with life and color and it isn't because a politician signed a paper and said they could. But when the time comes, they wither up and drop their leaves, lose their color and become silent. No one can stop that, either.

And so is the story of our lives. God moves through nature—and souls—like a whisper on water and he cannot be held back. Life shoots up straight out of death and no one can make it stop. An artist lives in the midst of this wonder, breathes it in, moves around in it, uncovers her unique contribution to it, and offers it back up to God.

The Wonder of Being a Poem

I stare out my window at the colors of fall, the last of the red leaves holding on tight. I'm thankful for their stubbornness because as soon as they fall, they'll turn, wither, and disappear.

The sun sinks low behind the Japanese maple and I watch as the sky turns from pale blue to pink streaks to a deep veiled gray. The way of the moon in the darkening winter sky reaches inside me with the pressure of ten thousand flower petals: something light and beautiful, but enough of them and you have yourself a very heavy weight.

What if I approached my life the way I look at the moon, with mystery and longing and a weight that is both beautiful and terrifying at the same time? The pattern and poetry of the moon undo me. This moon that moves through space and time in the pattern of seasons we can count on. And yet, she holds within her a mystery that cannot be touched or figured out.

Like the moon, the flow of a poem is at once mysterious as well as rhythmic. There are symbols stressed and unstressed, movement that flows yet is also predictable like the waves of the ocean that come in and push out, knowable yet each tide a little different. The moon phases in a pattern, but an image of the moon each month on the same day will look slightly different according to the temperature, the color of the sand and sky, and the mood of the one behind the camera.

Even in the simplest poems the little ones sing, ones of roses red and violets blue, the children know where to push and where to pull back, how to make a song. They hear the rhythm, practice, repeat—in and out like the tides, wax and wane like the moon, inhale and exhale like a breath.

We are created to live rhythmically in the rhythms of creation. Seven days repeated in a sequence of four weeks place us in the rhythm of the twenty-eight-day phases of the moon circling the earth. This lunar rhythm gets repeated twelve times in the annual sweep of earth and moon around the sun. These large encompassing rhythms call forth regularities of spring births, summer growth, autumn harvest, and winter sleep. Creation time is rhythmic. We are immersed in rhythms.

But we are also composed of rhythms. Physiologically we live out rhythms of pulse and breath. Our hearts beat steadily, circulating our blood through our bodies in impulses of sixty or eighty or a hundred times a minute. Our lungs expand

and contract, pushing oxygen through our bodies fifteen or twenty or thirty times a minute.

The interesting thing about rhythm is that we can slow down or quicken the tempo, but we cannot eliminate the beat, the cadence. This can be realized most readily in music and dance, but the very creation itself is this way. This is the nature of the creation of which we are part. We are embedded in time, but time is also embedded in us.[5]

Eugene Peterson, *Christ Plays in Ten Thousand Places*

Time is embedded in us. There is a wonder to time on earth. We have been placed on land, bound up in time, wound up to spin—like the moon, like the waves, like a *poem*.

How are we to live like a poem in an un-poetic world? How do we cooperate with the Spirit of God in the midst of uncooperative circumstance?

What if we approached the critic, our jobs, the kids at our table with the same wonder and anticipation an artist has when she approaches the canvas? What if we decided to believe our purpose in this world really is to reflect the glory of God?

Would we begin to see ourselves as wildly free, to approach the universe—the meal plan, the work project, the yard sale, our neighbor, the roof leak, the doctor appointment, the eternal destiny of our children—to approach it all with a wide-eyed wonder, with an edge-of-your-seat breath, with an expectation that *any minute* God will show himself in a way we have not yet seen? And he'll likely do it through *us*?

When we embrace the beauty of our design, when we recognize that he has made us to be unique expressions of himself, when we receive the gifts he has equipped us with and have the courage to pour them out, we worship. What else would it be?

Dare to get a sense of yourself in the world, as you live and breathe and *are*—if it's true that in him you have your being, in him you move and exist, then you have value and weight, not the kind of weight you want to lose and get rid of. The kind that makes it possible for you to move into the world with courage, security, as if you know you have something to offer and where your life comes from.

The deepest truth we are all to reveal is the full glory of God, no matter how we feel, who we're with, or what's gone wrong.

Today as we face our dishes, our proposals, our classrooms full of the future; as we sit to create, to write, and to live on purpose, may the promise of growth outweigh our fear of stumbling.

May we remember how swiftly perfect love drives out fear. May we know what it means to make art with our hands, in our souls, with our lives. May our "thousand brilliant excuses" spin around into one brilliant act of belief.[6]

12

create

Creative work is not a selfish act or a bid for attention on the part of the actor. It's a gift to the world and every being in it. Don't cheat us of your contribution. Give us what you've got.

—Steven Pressfield, *The War of Art*

Friends were here last night and we sat with socked feet on our sofa. We talked about the real and the gritty, about the fears and the whys of our faith. We prayed for belief, shared the serious and the not so much. And as I sat, the low-grade anxiety I had been living with began to slow. The whirring in my heart began to quiet. And the body of Christ showed up in these people as they expressed themselves, but also him—the mystery of Christ in us, our hope.

You read these words now, you who bear witness to truth. Soon, you will get up and make art in your worlds. My friends in my living room last night, they did the same thing. It is beautiful, all of it.

I see a rerun of *The Office*, the one where Ryan said his New Year's resolution was to live his life like it's an art project. I smile at the sarcasm, know the writers are making some kind of statement about that. It should be true even if they are making fun of it, *the art project life*. Every moment is packed with artistic possibility because, as an image bearer with a job to do, there is potential to reveal the glory of God in every circumstance, no matter how I feel, who I'm with, what my hands hold, or what's gone wrong. *God with us* lives *within us*. And he will come out through us in a million little ways.

The Creative Work of the Artists among Us

We're thinking about switching banks, and it's because of an artist. We've been with the big company bank for years, never thought we'd switch. But then, they were bought out by an even bigger company and fees and charges and stuff started happening. We went with it for a while, mainly because of Mark.

Mark is a young guy who worked at the big company bank, but he made it feel not so big-company. He answered the questions we actually had rather than constantly trying to get us to do banker-y things.

But then, Mark left. The void was obvious. We found out Mark was now working at the small-town bank down the road. And so we set up an appointment with him there, and I asked him why we should stay with the big company bank instead of following him to the small-town (but still FDIC-approved) bank. "Their technology is way better," he said. "We can't match it, at least not yet." And then, as he spoke, his computer froze up and he couldn't get it to work.

I could tell he was flustered, could tell he hated the fact that just as he said his small-town bank technology couldn't compete with the big guys, his little computer decided to prove it. So we kept talking, and we asked Mark why he left the big bank. He relaxed a bit and said that even though he did his good work at the big bank, he didn't feel as if he were a part of something bigger than himself. He wanted to be a part of the community where he lived, a part of a bigger whole. He said it with humility and grace and conviction. And as his computer sat frozen in the background, we connected with Mark in the now.

We aren't considering a switch because of what he said, but because of what he did even before he said it. "But he's just a banker!" you say, "and he's just trying to be a good one." Yes, but that's what also makes him an artist.

Art is too important a term to be used just for painters. And sculptors. And playwrights. And actors. And architects of a certain type. No, I think we need to broaden it to graphic designers and salespeople and bosses. To lay preachers, to gifted politicians and occasionally, to the guy who sweeps the floor. Art is a human act, something that's done with the right sort of intent. Art is when we do work that matters, in a creative way, in a way that touches them and changes them for the better.[1]

Seth Godin, Graceful

I recently watched a woman at the frozen yogurt shop move through her required tasks efficiently. She greeted people who came in the store, cleaned up messes behind them. John commented, "She works like she owns the place." I thought to myself, *She works like an artist.*

I don't know if she owned the place and working at the yogurt shop was her dream job or if she just needed the money to make rent. It didn't really matter. She was present in those moments when we saw her and seemed to have an awareness of something bigger than herself. She chose to do her job in a way that moved beyond the simple work of her hands to create an environment in the shop that was welcoming. It was a place I wanted to be.

Both Mark and the woman at the yogurt shop made art in their own way because they did their work in a way that made a difference, in a way that influenced the people around them. Your work can do that too.

Create in the Midst of Fear

Living like an artist rather than a technician can be terrifying. With the decision comes an admission that you are not in control, you may not have the answers, and your life no longer belongs to you. It doesn't matter if your art is a relationship, a job, a hobby, or some other desire of your heart, when it comes to doing a creative work, fear can be a powerful and abusive motivator. But the answer isn't to get rid of the fear.

Fear can also be a valuable teacher and I don't want it to go away. The goal isn't to push fear away forever; it's to refuse to be pushed around by fear at all. We have to remember that if we avoid the fear, we miss the art too. Fear doesn't go away just because you're doing that thing you love.

> Henry Fonda was still throwing up before each stage performance, even when he was seventy-five. In other words, fear doesn't go away. The warrior and the artist live by the same code of necessity, which dictates that the battle must be fought anew every day.[2]
>
> Steven Pressfield, The War of Art

Fear will be a threat whenever you set out to pursue a desire that means something to you. We all stand backstage with a puking Henry Fonda, ready to head out on Broadway. The fear is big, but the art is bigger.

When it gets hard, remember your image-bearing identity. You have been given power. You have been given love. You have been given a sound mind. Though fear is present, the spirit of fear does not live within you. The Spirit of God does.[3]

Create Even When It's Hard

It's 7:45 at night. The house is quiet except for the rain, and I tap out the rest of chapter 7 just as the cloud cover begins to lift. The trees are black against a barely lit sky. I consider how fast time flies when you're making art.

Ideas show up like welcome guests in brightly colored dresses. They nod their heads and curtsy their skirts and greet me like kind, new friends waiting to come alive in my company. They are delighted by my attention.

It's time to stop, finished or not. This time, I meet my personal deadline for the day. I gather up the laundry, fold it in front of *Pride & Prejudice* (the Keira Knightly version, but still good company). I settle in to the warm couch, content to be alone with my pillows and my thoughts. I think about my word count today. I am pleased with the direction. I eat ice cream and grin.

But this isn't normal, which is why it's so delightful. Still, it happens sometimes, fuel to keep me going in the midst of what *is* normal.

Normal creation is more like being pregnant. Pregnancy is hard and the days are long. When we see something that delights us, in art or in life, it is usually a result of the consistent, sacrificial, nonromantic effort of an artist. A daily commitment to showing up, to loving with actions and not just words, to repenting from the desperate shape of her flesh—a commitment to writing bad songs, awful words, uninspiring colors on the canvas—a commitment to morning sickness and living with saltine crumbs in the bottom of her purse.

One masterpiece is the work of ten thousand rough drafts. Every moment isn't packed with delight, inspiration, or hope. The dark days are heavy and they should be. *You carry something living inside you. There will be pain to get it out.*

I chase three Advil down with cold coffee. It's another writing day, but the ideas don't know it. They packed up their sparkly bags last Thursday and headed off to Tuscany, stuffing all of my passion and heart into those zipped-up bags, tucking away my easy words deep into their pockets.

But I'm a professional, and I no longer wait for ideas to return from long vacations. Instead, I show up, sit in my chair, face the day, fight the pull of the internet, ignore the dust on the baseboards, and I work. The resistance is in full force, pushing hard against my desire for progress.

I type out fifty-seven words and they are all ridiculous. For a moment I fear death, because I have written these words and someone may find them when I'm gone and think I was serious. *Erase them, and fast!* But I don't, because then I will have nothing to show for the work. I begin to type *I have nothing more to say* just to see the word count go up. I know I'll have to start over. I feel discouraged. Cry a little. Keep on writing. Check my email. Wash the dishes. Look at the oven. Think about dinner. Cry again. I fail to meet my personal deadline for the day. But it's time to stop, finished or not.

I pray for the Lord to redeem the time. I believe he can, I have doubts he will. But then I remember that he's done it before. Still, no day of writing is wasted, even a bad one. The same goes for living.

All you can do is remember the shape of your design, surrender yourself to a relentless pursuit of the art, then do it again tomorrow—no matter what circumstance you face.

The writing day is finished and I call my sister to let her know we're coming early to her house. I feel her excitement through the phone. We live only two hours up I-85, but we still don't see them often enough.

She says she can't wait to go grocery shopping for our visit and she isn't pretending. Where some may be annoyed that we plan to come earlier than expected, she is genuinely glad.

She loves having people over. There is no hint of mere polite excitement. She doesn't have that in her.

We arrive to an imperfectly beautiful home, dog runs out the door as soon as we open it, kids race upstairs for games of fort-building and dare. She calls us to the kitchen, salsa bowl filled up as high as our hopes for connection. It's easy here.

Her art comes out when she hosts. Not because she makes it perfect but because it makes her come alive. What is most alive in her is poured out and wakes something up within us.

It's a month later and I'm having ten people to our house on Saturday night. I'm nervous about it even though I enjoy people, food, and company. But it isn't the most natural thing for me to be in charge of a dinner party. Party planning doesn't show up on the list of my gifts when I take those career tests.

Still, I do it. Not because I'm good at it but because the deeper purpose behind it is something that makes me come alive. Dr. Crabb talks about how true spiritual community happens when believers learn to turn our chairs toward one another, dare to look each other in the eyes, and search for what is alive there. Not to dissect the pain or the hurt, although that will be there. But to dig for the glimpses of joy, of life, and where Jesus wants to show up alive in us.

It doesn't feel particularly true right now, but I know Jesus wants to show up alive in me on Saturday night with a houseful of friends. But before he can show up in me, I have to show up in my own life, in the midst of a circumstance that might make me uncomfortable. It isn't natural for me to have so many over at once, but for me right now, I know it's right. I might rather choose a few over a crowd, but living like an artist doesn't mean doing only those things we love on the surface. It may mean learning to see beyond the obvious, beyond my own personal comfort, and pursuing the desire that lies beneath.

It may take extra time and belief, but at the deepest part of who I am, I long to connect, to engage. I want to know and to be known. And sometimes for that to happen, I have to invite groups over for connection and tacos. When I show up for the glory of God and the benefit of others, art comes out.

My friend Kendra cooks. And it isn't just about the food, it's about what the food means for family. She is so passionate about it that she wanted to share that passion with people. She opened her own business and began to teach cooking classes. She was good at it, and people who took one class usually ended up taking two. Because when Kendra is in the kitchen, she creates. She is free. She makes art. And she inspires others to make art as well.

A few years after she started her business, Kendra had a baby and it became more difficult for her to teach the classes. The business began to feel like a burden a little bit. So she listened to desire, to the Lord, and to her people, and she decided to shut it down. And you know what?

She still makes art. It just looks different now.

Every day, she shows up and cooks for her husband and mothers that baby with love and fullness and hope. She isn't perfect, she doesn't always feel loving and creative, but she loves anyway and makes smart decisions for her family. She bears the image of God and she has a job to do.

So do you. For some people, it might look like starting a business while for others it looks like shutting one down. For some it might look like hosting a party with ease while for others it looks like hosting a party with struggle. There's no way to predict what might happen when an artist chooses to show up and create.

Create Space

There's a phone commercial on TV where a man in a suit asks a group of grade school kids, "Is it better to do one thing at a time or two things at once?" And they all shout together and raise their hands, "Two things at once!"

When I first saw it, I thought it was a joke. Clearly it's better to do just one thing at a time. Trying to do two things at once is what makes me crazy. When I have to do two things at once, it may as well be two hundred things. It feels impossible to do either thing well.

The phone company makes a point: when it comes to your phone service, it's better to do two things at once, like talk on the phone and look up a restaurant. But in real life, the opposite is true. When we are trying to do too many things at once, we can't move into the world as we fully are because we simply don't have time—we aren't living, we're surviving, from one thing to the next. Whether it's creating a chapter of a book or a quiet conversation, trying to do too many things at once is one of my biggest obstacles to living artfully.

A friend shares a difficult struggle. Tears well up in her eyes as she talks. The pain runs deep, maybe more than she even knows. I'm aware of my desire to be helpful, to make it better, to offer some words of hope. As I listen to my own discomfort because of my inability to help her, I realize I'm thinking more of me than of her. Is it possible to stay my attention on the person I'm with more than perseverate on what my response will be to her? Is it possible to do just one thing at a time?

Unmoving and still listening, I offer my discomfort up to the Lord. She continues to communicate the details of her pain. I confront all of my own mixed motives, my own self-reliant tendency as I listen, and am able to privately offer them up as they come to mind. I desperately want to be a technician in this—what is the *right* thing to say?

As I silently confess my addiction to usefulness, I recognize a new obsession: a deep desire to know her, to hear what she is saying now, to learn something I didn't know before.

The earlier question *how can I help her?* is changing into a new question, *how can I see her?* How will Immanuel show himself right now, not just for her in her pain but for me in my self-obsession? *God with us* is big enough to handle us both.

When I release my obsession with finding a cure, I can embrace the desire to be curious. This person, this friend, is not a project or an assignment. She is an image bearer, a lyric, a poem. The color of her pain runs dark and she needs some time to face it. This is holy ground, and her process can't be rushed, dissected, or figured out. For me to be an artist in this moment means to create space for this conversation to have room to breathe.

Am I willing to let her be a mystery?

Am I willing to sit beside her without giving in to the pressure to fix her?

Am I willing to let her wrestle without quoting Scripture or forcing prayer?

Am I willing to walk away more uncomfortable and with more questions than when we began?

The degree to which I can say yes to these questions may be the extent to which I can reflect the glory of God as an artist in my community. When people are hurting, searching, and in difficult places, they don't want me with my bag filled with skills. They don't want me to rush to solutions. They simply want me as I am, where I am, fully alive.

If you are a surgeon or a dentist, we want your bag of skills. Use your training and your technique on me, I've got a cavity. But if you are a friend, leave your bag at the door. I don't need an expert. I need an artist. I need someone who will be willing to show up and let me be a mystery, someone who will appreciate me as a fellow image bearer, someone who looks to Jesus as their ultimate security and doesn't need me to be okay so they'll feel better.

I long for someone to be willing to ask me questions, not for the sake of knowing the answer, but for the delight of knowing *me*.[4]

> The more I think it over, the more I feel that there is nothing more truly artistic than to love people.[5]
>
> Vincent Van Gogh

Create Generously

The violinist, the professional musician in the corner of the nursery, seemed to have a respect for his art that I didn't understand. He wasn't trying to further his career by playing for those babies. He was simply gifting his art, being who he was in the presence of others. He was entrusted with a sacred task and he was not in charge of it. He was a *steward* of it. These words from Michael Card come to mind:

> Artists in medieval times did not sign their work. It never occurred to them to do so. . . . Their art was a gift meant to point away from themselves and toward the God who gave it. They were safely hidden in Christ, free from the tyranny of the self. They knew the great truth that they were nothing more and nothing less than children of a great King who had been entrusted with a sacred task: to win praise for their Lord. Knowing who we are is the hiddenness of humility. It is believing that the giftedness we may indeed possess is not of our own making, that the purpose of its being given is not that we might gain attention or praise for ourselves, but that we might respond in gratitude with our best creative effort to win praise for the One who first gave the gift.[6]

It was a Monday when several friends and family members were gathered at my sister's house. They were helping me with a video project for my first book and we took a break for lunch.

As I tried not to spill salsa on my pants, I overheard a conversation between my dad and my friend Reeve about music and songwriting. He works in radio and she's a musician, so they had some mutual interests. He asked if she wrote her own songs.

She said she did and then he asked her what kinds of things she liked to write about. They talked for a few more minutes, and then he said this: *Would you play a little something for us now?*

Her face turned red and she smiled small, shrugged her shoulders and looked around the room. Was she waiting for someone to object? No one did.

We had the time and my brother-in-law had an old guitar. She settled in to her place on the sofa and we continued to eat as she began to strum. Time stopped a little and we held our breath. In the span of four minutes, Reeve took us on a trip into her soul. We were quiet at the end simply because we hadn't come back yet.[7]

She could have said no to playing for us, but I think she would have regretted it. We would have regretted it too. When an artist chooses to be generous, everyone wins. Even though she wrote the song about her own life, we could all somehow relate to it.

The more personal you are with your art, the more generally it applies to those who are there to receive it. It seems counterintuitive, I know. Add more of yourself to your work—more of your personality, preferences, and desire. Reject your fear of scarcity, of sharing and competition. Instead, delight us with what you have to offer. Choose generosity and share the unique shape of your design. Offer yourself as you are, not as you wish you were. The more we see you, the more we'll see ourselves. Releasing the art alive within you is about waking up to God and responding in worship. This is vital to a thriving community and is often closely related with our life stage and perspective.

Last night before I went to bed, I turned on the news to check the weather. I rarely do this before bed and I quickly remembered why.

There was a breaking-news bulletin on the bottom of the screen and the newscaster announced four children were missing one county over. When he mentioned the ages of the children, my heart sank—they were the same age as my son. It was late, they were already missing for hours, and the temperature was dropping.

I couldn't sleep thinking of them, so I prayed in the dark before drifting off. I prayed from a frightening place within me, the place of a mother imagining those children as my own. This morning, I checked as soon as I woke up and was relieved to discover those children were found. They had wandered off into the woods while playing, and now they are safe at home.

It obviously doesn't always turn out so beautifully. I could have prayed just as fervently and woken up to a tragic result. But the point is, I was moved with compassion to pray because of my life stage right now. If the children had been a different age, it would have affected me, but I may not have taken it as personally. Everyone has their own unique passions as well as their distinct burdens. We are responsible to pay attention to what moves us and respond in faith. The body of Christ grows when each member gives what they have to give—that applies not only to our gifting but also to our burdens. What breaks your heart might not break mine. You are not responsible to convince me to change, you are responsible to be generous in the areas you feel called to.

Offer what you have in the presence of others.

Pray over what breaks your heart in the presence of God.

Create with Courage

I'm eight years old and we live on a tiny plot of land in the block between Gladstone Avenue and Meridian Street.

Our house sits on her foundation there and smells of lemon, bacon, and a rainy day. Two bedrooms and one bath seem perfectly fine to me, and our family of four will live in this little white house with the gravel drive for eleven years.

A thousand warm miles of tree-climbing, sprinkler-splashing, Barbie-playing days stretch out in front of us. June in Indiana wears gauzy pink dresses and a promise in her eyes. Endless space fills up kid days, the cicadas and the ice cream truck sing summer's song together.

The morning dew and the mourning dove frame those summer memories like a mama's warm arms around a girl who knows she is loved. But as much as I want to paint my childhood in carefree shades of sun-kissed cheeks, the truth is my kid days were filled with lots of worry.

I worried about school starting back up, tornados, and robbers. I worried about what if our car rolled out of the driveway while we were sleeping? What if our house catches on fire while we're gone? What if E.T. lives in my closet? Is it really possible to spontaneously combust?

We were made by the hands of a Maker to be brave, to take heart and have courage. But we get good at the things we practice, and instead of scales of courage, I played dark melodies of fear.

We don't have to teach kids to be afraid. They come by it all on their own.

Recently I had a dream that a high-up executive called and wanted me to join a Very Big Tour of Speakers. In my waking hours I've never had much of a desire to be part of a tour of speakers, much less a Very Big one. When I woke up and realized it was a dream, I took a little time to figure the dream out.

205

I once heard someone say when we dream, the main thing to pay attention to isn't so much every detail and what it all means. But the overall *feeling* of the dream could give us a hint into something we're dealing with in our waking life.

The feeling that lingered with me when I woke up from that particular dream was obvious—it was the feeling of being picked.

Sometimes don't we just want to be picked? It's true God picks me. But there is sometimes a disconnect for me between God picking me as a child he loves and God empowering me to make an impact in the world around me.

Seth Godin hosted a day gathering in Tribeca last summer and it had a simple, two-word theme for attendees. *Pick Yourself.*

"Once you understand that there are problems just waiting to be solved, once you realize that you have all the tools and all the permission you need, then opportunities to contribute abound. No one is going to pick you. Pick yourself."[8]

It's an important message to me. Because even though I know my identity as a believer is solid in Christ, if I don't decide to believe it for myself, then it won't impact the way I love, the way I live, or the way I work. I may be able to be effective and even successful in the world's eyes, but until I pick myself, I'm not sure I will be truly making art with my life.

When I filter that statement through the reality of my life in Christ, it becomes even more powerful. Have I been given a spirit of power, love, and a sound mind? Am I an image bearer? Do I have a job to do? Then what else could I possibly be waiting for?

Now it isn't doubt or critics or lack of something to offer that is keeping you from creating. It's time to call your hesitancy what it is: *you're procrastinating*. And it's time to stop.

In his book *The War of Art*, Steven Pressfield says this about procrastination: "Procrastination is the most common manifestation of Resistance because it's the easiest to rationalize. We don't tell ourselves, 'I'm never going to write my symphony.' Instead we say, 'I'm going to write my symphony; I'm just going to start tomorrow.'"[9]

Don't wait until tomorrow. Pick yourself today. You already have everything you need. Embrace the art alive within you, and believe in the little ways God wants to release his art into the world through you.

Let's pick up the pen, the pan, the brush. Let's open our eyes, our hands, our hearts. Let's see fear and then laugh in his face because somebody has to. Why not let it be us? Let's carry on together.

We Will Make Art

It's December 31, 2010. I sit at home alone with my thoughts and my laptop. John is at the church, ringing in the New Year with a few hundred students, his tenth year as a youth pastor. I'm home with our sleeping kids.

I piddle around on Twitter, watch Ryan Seacrest and his frosted tips introduce various singers before the ball drops. I check my email more out of instinct than necessity. There is a message from my friend Annie Downs waiting in my inbox, and when I realize she is online, we write back and forth a few times.

It's like texting for old people.

My first book is due to release in the fall of 2011 and here we are on the last day of 2010. I am terrified about what the coming year will hold, desperate to stay hidden and safe at home, worried what might happen when my innermost thoughts are available to any stranger's whim and fancy. It feels like a big deal.

I live with a low-grade anxiety about the coming year, deeply aware of my desire to find a manual that tells me just exactly how to release a book, be a mom, make the dinner, love my neighbor, and breathe all at the same time. When I get nervous, I grasp for how-tos.

Annie knows all of this—I am scared, 2011 is a big deal, and writing is equal parts thrilling and terrifying. She just released a book of her own, so she knows perhaps better than most. But instead of saying, "I'm terrified, aren't you? Let's hop a plane to Fiji, m'kay?" she says something that will forever change the way I see my life and the way I'm choosing to live it.

Want to know what she says?

"2011: We will make art."

It isn't much, and I don't think she means to be profound about it. But when I read those five words, the guest I don't even know I'm waiting for finally shows up to the party: *courage*. There he stands like an old friend, sure and confident as ever. It feels like a tiny revolution is born right here in my heart as I sit in my cookie monster jammy pants with my hair knotted on top of my head.

New Year's Eve 2010 was about more than just the book I had coming out. It felt bigger than that. It was the first step toward waking up to living honestly, to sharing my life with others through writing, connection, and a common fear, joy, and delight. Even though it was only through email, Annie sat with me in my anxiety. She recognized my fear and didn't advise me or Bible-verse it away. She walked with me toward courage and included herself in my struggle.

We will make art took me out of myself that night, escorting me into a bigger story. Receiving those words from her felt more necessary to my well-being as a person than making a list, a resolution, or a plan for the year would have felt in that moment.

It was also, in a way I can't fully explain, somehow connected to that cold night in Michigan so many years ago. Sarah's music and the generosity with which she shared it came back to me as Annie's words penetrated something deep within me, something of hope and freedom that God made with his hands and put within all of us. From that day on, art started seeping in from every crack in the wall, from every eye and hand I daily encountered, from every prayer and tree and common meal.

I began to hear, not only the words people said, but the way in which they said them. When a friend talked about a project at work or their unborn baby or their excitement over cheese and wine, I saw something more than just the thing they mentioned. I began to notice the influence of people who were at least partially in touch with what made them come alive. Likewise, I also noticed the discouragement and frustration of people who denied they had anything to offer at all. I began to notice the disclaimers people put on their deepest desires. Their disclaimers poked me awake and pulled at a thread inside of me. This book is that thread unraveled to the fullest extent.

Annie's words—we will make art—meant something to me not because I'm creative but because I'm *human*. I hope by now that phrase means something to you as well. You know creating is more than paint and clay and lyrics. You know there is an art alive within you and the work you do to uncover it is not a waste of time. You are an image bearer and that is not about you becoming famous or important or promoted but about you becoming more fully yourself for the glory of God. And when you are fully yourself, everyone benefits.

You are an image bearer and you have a job to do.

Here is your job description:

Desire. Be brave enough to acknowledge what you most long for and be willing to expose desires in the light of the love of God.

Rescue the sleeping desires of childhood, not as answers *to* life but as evidence *of* life. Allow the uncovering to lead you to the shape of your soul.

Sink into the depths of God, knowing he created the world and re-creates you. And from that re-creation of you comes co-creation with Christ. You cannot do anything on your own.

See how the critics carry their gifts, not just those with sharp tongues and narrowed eyes, but the critics of circumstance and shattered dreams and disappointment. These remind you where your true strength comes from—not the admiration of man or the thrill of success or even the sweet delight of a good day. Your true strength comes from the absolute fact that you have been crucified with Christ. And Christ has authority over fear, failure, and death. So even as you die, you live.

Listen to the way God speaks through your tears, your questions, your heartbreak. He meets you through the ordinary gifts on a Tuesday, and shows up in your crazy ideas. Consider how what you hear reveals evidence of your unique design.

Show up and be who you already are, with your limits as well as your potentials. Show up with your hands out and your eyes open, willing to receive the day as it is and not as you wish it were. You are a poem with a rhythm all your own.

Wait. Remember creativity begins and ends with *waiting*. Wait in faith for the movement of God—even when it hurts and you don't see results.

Offer what you have in the presence of another—no matter how small or weak it may seem to you.

Wonder. In his book *Souvenirs of Solitude,* Brennan Manning asks this question: "Have I grown uncomfortable with the fact that Jesus tells us to model our lives after flowers and birds?" Don't be offended that Jesus points to petals and wings and growing things. Be *relieved*.

And finally, *create* as if it were your highest calling. Take the bread and the wine and remember Jesus who did only what he saw his Father do. Take the basin and the towel and remember one another. Create space in the way you wash the feet and generously love your neighbor, the way you speak to your family and those at your table. Create with courage and with faith.

As the poetry of God, all our hands make a different kind of art and we create with our successes and our failures, our talents and our shortcomings, our instruments and our yard rakes, our numbers and our calloused hands. Nothing is off-limits.

The Artist's Manifesto

We are the mothers, the lovers, the nighttime storytellers. We are the hopers, the fathers, the harmonizers. We are the visionaries, the silent supporters, the leaders, and the background singers.

We are the servants, the musicians, and the politicians; the waiters, the washers, and the obstetricians. We are the thinkers and we are the believers.

We are the dust and the brushstroke, the poets and the poetry, the weak empowered, the broken made whole.

We are the mirrors of God on earth, the megaphones of glory, the hands and eyes and hearts of heaven.

We are grieved but not hopeless, brought from darkness into light, given a new name, a new future, a new Power alive within us.

God is the Artist and he has made us.

We are his poem and we will make art.

acknowledgments

To these I offer a humble thank-you:

John, I am speechless when I think of you. If my words inspire anyone in a way that moves them toward making art, it's only because your words first moved me.

To Myquillyn, the sister who reminds me not to take myself too seriously—you consistently teach me how to find my brave yes and my strong no.

To Annie, Kendra, and Melissa—you remind me why I do this.

To Mom and Dad, Dr. Larry Crabb, and Steve Lynam—thank you for nudging me one step closer to fully released courage in ways you may never know. Your influence is so much a part of my life that I can't begin to credit you for all the truth I've learned from each of you.

To my editor, Andrea Doering—I especially thank you for not accepting the first draft of this book.

To Esther Fedorkevich, my agent who has championed these words from the very beginning—thank you for believing long before I did.

To The Thinklings, the writers at (in)courage, and the readers of *Chatting at the Sky*—I am grateful for your support, encouragement, questions, notes, and the art you make with your words and your lives.

notes

Chapter 1 Awake

1. Seth Godin, *Graceful* (New York: New Word City, Inc., 2010), Kindle ebook. This is a short, 32-page ebook. Seth Godin is an entrepreneur, bestselling author, and creator of the most popular marketing blog in the world written by a single person.

Part 2 Uncover the Art You Were Born to Make

1. Makoto Fujimura, interview with Becky Garrison, "Artists Are Catalysts," *The High Calling*, Feb. 24, 2009, http://www.thehighcalling.org/work/artists-are-catalysts-interview-makoto-fujimura-part-2#.Ua3g97-TPu1.

Chapter 3 Desire: Look Within

1. Ruth Haley Barton, *Sacred Rhythms* (Downers Grove, IL: InterVarsity, 2006), 25.
2. Natalie Goldberg, *Writing Down the Bones* (Boston: Shambhala, 1986), 8.
3. Barton, *Sacred Rhythms*, 23.
4. Barbara Brown Taylor, *An Altar in the World* (New York: Harper One, 2009), 110.
5. Timothy Keller, *Every Good Endeavor* (New York: Dutton, 2012), 36.

Chapter 4 Rescue: Look Back

1. Jon Acuff, *Quitter* (Brentwood, TN: Lampo Press, 2011), 34.
2. Gary Morland, *From Beer to Eternity: A Little Story of Addiction and Beyond* (self-published, August 2, 2012). This is an ebook my dad wrote—his own journey of alcoholism and salvation.

3. I wrote a post on my blog about that day in the Compassion office, reading the "My Plan for Tomorrow" booklets the children wrote. You can read that post here: http://www.chattingatthesky.com/2011/06/02/how-stickers-can-change-the-world-day-4/.

4. C. S. Lewis, *The Weight of Glory* (New York: Macmillan, 1949), 4–6.

Chapter 5 Sink: Look Up

1. Madeleine L'Engle, *Walking on Water* (Wheaton: Harold Shaw, 1980), 134.

2. See John 13.

3. John 13:14–15 NASB.

4. J. E. Conant, *Every Member Evangelism* (Philadelphia: Sunday School Times Co., 1922), 60.

5. The following Scripture references in this section are taken from John 14:3–6 NASB.

6. "7503. Raphah," accessed June 5, 2013, http://biblesuite.com/hebrew/7503.htm.

7. Shaun Groves, "Downward Mobility," *Shaun Groves*, May 24, 2012, http://shaungroves.com/2012/05/downward-mobility/.

8. N. D. Wilson, *Notes from the Tilt-A-Whirl* (Nashville: Thomas Nelson, 2009), 33.

Chapter 6 See: Look Around

1. Oswald Chambers, *Bread and Wine* (New York: Orbis Books, 2005), 30–31.

2. Elisa Rice, "John Mayer 2011 Clinic—Manage the Temptation to Publish Yourself," *Berklee Blogs,* July 11, 2011, http://www.berklee-blogs.com/2011/07/john-mayer-2011-clinic-manage-the-temptation-to-publish-yourself/.

3. L'Engle, *Walking on Water*, 70.

Chapter 7 Listen: Look Beneath

1. L'Engle, *Walking on Water*, 19.

2. Charles Martin, *When Crickets Cry* (Nashville: Westbow, 2006), ix.

3. Henri J. M. Nouwen, *Here and Now* (New York: Crossroad Publishing, 1994), 59.

4. If you are interested in reading the posts I refer to in this chapter or learning more about my trip to the Philippines with Compassion International, visit http://www.chattingatthesky.com/compassion.

5. Brené Brown, *The Gifts of Imperfection* (Center City, MN: Hazelden, 2010), 72–73.

6. Goldberg, *Writing Down the Bones*, 55.

Part 3 Release the Art You Were Made to Live

1. Mark Batterson, *The Circle Maker* (Grand Rapids: Zondervan, 2011), 76.

Chapter 8 Show Up

1. G. K. Chesterton, *Orthodoxy* (Chicago: Moody, 2009), 31–32.
2. Parker Palmer, *Let Your Life Speak* (San Francisco: Jossey-Bass, 2000), 55.
3. Steven Pressfield, *The War of Art* (New York: Grand Central Publishing, 2002), 39.

Chapter 9 Wait

1. "Steven Tyler," *Oprah's Next Chapter*, OWN. Original airdate January 1, 2012.
2. Michael Card, *Scribbling in the Sand* (Downers Grove, IL: InterVarsity, 2002), 47.
3. Seth Godin, "Van Gogh Lost His Ear to Prove a Point," *Unleashing the Ideavirus* (Do You Zoom, Inc., 2001), installment 65 of 87. Seth Godin introduced the concept of books as souvenirs in this free e-book. I took that concept further to apply to all kinds of art we make.
4. See Zechariah 4:10.

Chapter 10 Offer

1. See Notes on the Bible by Albert Barnes, http://barnes.biblecommenter.com/matthew/14.htm.
2. Henri Nouwen, *Bread for the Journey* (New York: Harper Collins, 1997), June 21 entry.
3. Gary Morland, "Trust Looks Like," *New Life'n*, February 1, 2011, http://newlife919blog.blogs.com/new_life_919_blog/2011/02/trust-looks-like.html. Accessed December 8, 2012.
4. Larry Crabb, *Real Church* (Nashville: Thomas Nelson, 2009), 103.
5. Norman Grubb, *The Spontaneous You* (Fort Washington, PA: Christian Literature Crusade, 1966), 128.

Chapter 11 Wonder

1. Eugene Peterson, *Christ Plays in Ten Thousand Places* (Grand Rapids: Eerdmans, 2005), 52.
2. Ann Voskamp, *One Thousand Gifts* (Grand Rapids: Zondervan, 2010), 74.
3. Wilson, *Notes from the Tilt-A-Whirl*, 157.
4. Ibid.
5. Peterson, *Christ Plays in Ten Thousand Places*, 68.
6. This phrase, "a thousand brilliant excuses," comes from a line in Brennan Manning's book *Souvenirs of Solitude* (Colorado Springs: NavPress, 2009).

Chapter 12 Create

1. Godin, *Graceful*, from "Art? Is This Art?" chapter.
2. Pressfield, *War of Art*, 14.
3. See 2 Timothy 1:7.

4. This idea of having a spiritually forming conversation comes from a teaching by Larry Crabb in his School of Spiritual Direction, attended October 2012, Colorado Springs.

5. Fritz Erpel, *Van Gogh: The Self-Portraits* (New York: New York Graphic Society, 1969), 17.

6. Card, *Scribbling in the Sand*, 78–79.

7. Because we were there to film a video, this spontaneous moment was caught on camera. Watch an example of an artist being generous—Reeve Coobs singing her original song, "Night Owl": http://www.youtube.com/watch?v=z9yK5ZbWRJQ&feature=player_embeddedvideographer: Duane Harms.

8. Seth Godin, "Reject the Tyranny of Being Picked," *Seth Godin*, March 21, 2011, http://sethgodin.typepad.com/seths_blog/2011/03/reject-the-tyranny-of-being-picked-pick-yourself.html, accessed February 19, 2013.

9. Pressfield, *War of Art*, 21.

Emily P. Freeman is a writer who creates space for souls to breathe. Author of *Grace for the Good Girl: Letting Go of the Try-Hard Life,* she also created the blog *Chatting at the Sky,* is a regular contributor at DaySpring's (in)courage, and has traveled as an advocate for Compassion International. She attended Columbia International University to study the Bible and the University of North Carolina at Greensboro where she earned a degree in Educational Interpreting for the Deaf. She and her husband, John, live in North Carolina with their three children.

connect with
emily

• • •

emilypfreeman.com

EmilyFreemanAuthor

emilypfreeman

ChattingAtTheSky.com

"EMILY FREEMAN is one of those rare writers: profoundly biblical, lyrical, transparent—memorable. Her emancipating words on these pages offer the needed keys to all the good girls longing to take wing— and soar home to God's heart."

—ANN VOSKAMP, *New York Times* bestselling author of *One Thousand Gifts*

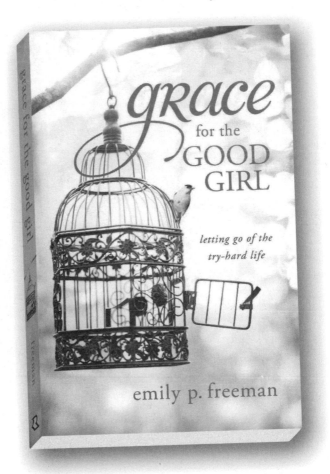

Share Emily's wisdom and encouragement with the young women in your life.

for young women

graceful

LETTING GO OF YOUR
TRY-HARD LIFE

emily p. freeman
AUTHOR OF *GRACE FOR THE GOOD GIRL*

If you've been struggling with expectations—from your parents, your teachers, your friends, and even yourself—*Graceful* is for you. Are you trying hard to catch up but aren't sure what it is you're chasing?

READ AND BE SET FREE.